MARGUERITE HENRY'S
All About
HORSES

MARGUERITE HENRY'S

All About

HORSES

WITH THREE COLOR PORTFOLIOS
AND WITH PHOTOGRAPHS BY
WALTER D. OSBORNE

 RANDOM HOUSE · NEW YORK

Unless otherwise credited, all photographs are by Walter Osborne.

New York Public Library: Prints Division, iv, xi; Courtesy of the American Museum of Natural History, 5, 6, 9, 10, 11, 12; Marc and Evelyn Bernheim, Rapho Guillumette Pictures, 14; Toni Angermayer, Photo Researchers, Inc., 17, 19; Emil Schulthess, Conzett & Huber, 20; British Museum, 24, 25, 26; The Metropolitan Museum of Art, 22 and 33 (left) (The Rogers Fund, 1915), 27, 29 (Bequest of William Milne Grinnell, 1920), 33 (right) (Gift of Alexander Smith Cochran, 1913); Marc Riboud, Magnum, 28; Courtesy, Museum of Fine Arts, Boston, John Coolidge Collection, 34; The American Museum of Natural History, Courtesy, American Heritage Publishing Co., Inc., 43; Fritz Henle, Monkmeyer, 52; Courtesy, Kennedy Galleries, Inc., 56; Lewis Watson, Monkmeyer, 73; Dodge Stables, Rochester, Michigan, 78.

The illustration on page 116 is from the book *A Leg at Each Corner,* written and illustrated by Norman Thelwell. Copyright © 1962 by Norman Thelwell. Published 1963 by E. P. Dutton and Co., Inc. Reproduced with their permission.

The illustrations on pages 38, 46, 49 and 55 are from *The Frederic Remington Book* by Harold McCracken. Copyright © 1966 by Harold McCracken. Used by permission of Doubleday & Company, Inc.

Contents

LIST OF ILLUSTRATIONS

All About

HORSES

Morgan mare and foal

In the Beginning

It was less than two million years ago, scientists tell us, that Man appeared upon the earth, but the horse was here long, long before that—fifty million years ago!

He looked very different from today's horse. If we could do a flashback, as they do in motion pictures, and meet this prehistoric creature, we would not even recognize him. He was small as a fox and he had heavy pads under his toes. But instead of running like a fox with a long, smooth-flowing stride, he had a choppy, up-down gait, more like a pig. His teeth, too, were piglike, and he nibbled on fern fronds and lush jungly leaves and small fruit.

If no living man ever saw this tiny horse, how do we know so much about him? Scientists literally dug up the facts, and that story is as exciting as a mystery thriller.

3

The man who stumbled upon the first clue was a brick-maker from Suffolk, England, named William Colchester. One day in the year 1838 he was digging clay and sand in his backyard when his spade upturned a tiny tooth. He could tell it was not a child's tooth, but he had no idea what creature it had belonged to. Being of a curious turn of mind, he sent the tooth off at once to the Geological Society in London.

Soon afterward an important member of the Society journeyed all the way to Suffolk to see Mr. Colchester. He, too, was puzzled by this tiny tooth. "Why not hire a bone-digger," he suggested, "a young boy to dig the earth in your yard? He might find more teeth—maybe jaws and skulls, too."

The brickmaker did take on a helper for a few pennies a week. The boy dug and dug and crumbled the clay and sifted the sand through his fingers and, sure enough, he came upon another clue. It was a piece of jaw this time, with a lone tooth attached.

Suddenly Mr. Colchester became more interested in bones than bricks. He himself went to London, carrying the strange fragment wrapped up as carefully as if he had found buried treasure—which in fact he had!

The scientists now were more baffled than ever. They called in Sir Richard Owen, an expert on prehistoric life. Sir Richard examined the structure of the jaw and the tiny tooth, and concluded they had once belonged to a monkey. Perhaps, he said, England had long ago been a jungle with monkeys chattering and screaming in the trees. His opinion was discussed at length in the scientific journals of the day.

Newsmen, however, pooh-poohed the idea. They thought it more likely that gypsies traveling through England years before had lost one of their monkeys, and all that was left of

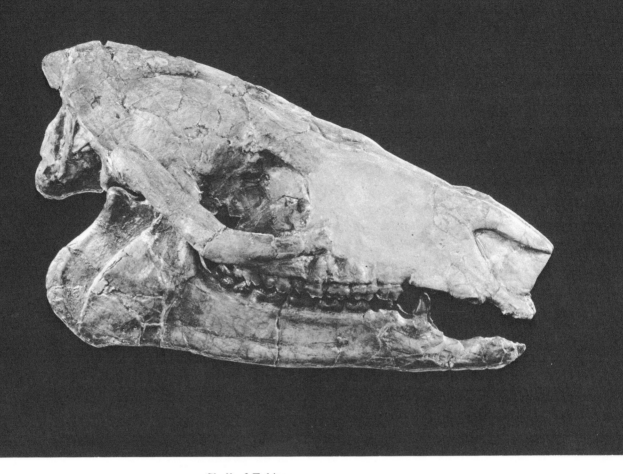

Skull of Eohippus

him was a few bones to prove it.

The mystery began to unravel when a second jaw was found in southern England a few months later. Almost the whole set of teeth was intact, and with this new fossil Sir Richard discarded the monkey idea. He identified it as belonging to a small animal who lived on leaves, whose eyes were big for his size, and whose feet, he guessed, were hoofed. He gave him a long handle of a name—*Hyracotherium*.

Some thirty years later in our own southwestern plains a similar fossil was discovered. This time it was American scientists who thought it had belonged to a monkey. But gradually they came to recognize that instead of a monkey it must have been a member of the Hyracotherium family. The Americans

5

went a step further; they identified him as the miniature ancestor of the horse.

The Dawn Horse

The illustration on this page is a painting of the first horse as well as we can reconstruct him. In real life, he stood about twelve inches high and had four toes on each front foot and three on each hind. Professor O. C. Marsh of Yale University chose for this early horse a simple name: *hippus,* which means horse, and *eo,* which means dawn. Together they make *Eohippus,* or dawn horse.

Eohippus was about the same size as a fox

One day the professor had a famous visitor from England. He was an authority on the whole animal kingdom, from jellyfishes to dinosaurs. He had come to America to lecture on the feet of fossil horses, and his name was Thomas Henry Huxley. The two men had a wonderful time comparing notes. The great Huxley was so impressed by the professor's collection of fossils that he asked for a scrap of paper, and right there and then he made a rough sketch of what he thought the first horse-creature looked like. He gave it a long body and head, tiny ears, and five toes on each foot. Then, with a chuckle, he put a long-armed, monkey-like man on the horse's back—even though he knew that man did not then exist—and he labeled him *Eohomo*, or dawn man.

While this sketch was made in fun, scientists later agreed that little Eohippus did have a five-toed ancestor much like Mr. Huxley's cartoon. They could tell this by a nubbin of bone they found above the four toes of early skeletons.

The World of Eohippus

If we could focus a powerful telescope on the world of fifty million years ago, we would be amazed at what our own continent looked like. We would see an immense swamp with ferns growing big as trees, and lizards and crocodiles slithering through the muck. Even as far north as Alaska the climate would be warm and wet with jungle foliage dripping heavy globs of water. This was the world of Eohippus, the dawn horse.

We don't know whether he had web feet or not, but it was a fine advantage to have, as he did, many toes. He could spread them as he ran along to keep from sinking into the boggy earth. We do know that his legs were short, so of course he could not travel very fast. When his enemies—fierce wolflike beasts—pursued him, he had to hide instead of run. But it was easy to disappear in the deep tropical forest.

At this stage in his history he was a browser, not a grazer. His teeth were just right for nibbling the soft leafy food he lived on. They were simple teeth, with low crowns, much like our own cheek teeth.

Mesohippus, the Middle Horse

Millions of years rolled on before any real changes occurred in the early horse, and these were only slight. Very gradually his legs grew a little longer and he lost a toe on each front foot, and the middle toe began to be more important. He stood taller now, about the size of a springer spaniel.

His face began to lengthen too, and his whole head increased in size. His eyes grew rounder, and instead of being close together, they were set wider apart and farther back. His teeth grew much bigger, and each row was continuous with only a little gap behind the front teeth where the bit now rests.

He was still a browser, living on tender twigs, leaves and fruits, and he is now known as *Mesohippus,* or "middle horse."

Spaniel-sized Mesohippus was beginning to look like today's horse

Merychippus, the Grass-Eater

In the next five million years dramatic changes were taking place on the face of the earth. Very very slowly the great plains were developing, forests were thinning out, mountains were building up, and between them grassy plains stretched endlessly where before there had been swampland. A whole new world—flat and wide and dry—was opening up.

Now our little horse had nowhere to hide from his enemies; he had to run away. This he managed by traveling on his middle toe, his side toes seldom touching the ground. By now he had grown bigger, as big as a small Shetland pony, and he could run almost as fast.

His eating habits changed, too. With his leafy food grown scarce, he was forced to eat the grass of the plains. He had to reach down now for his food, but this was no problem.

9

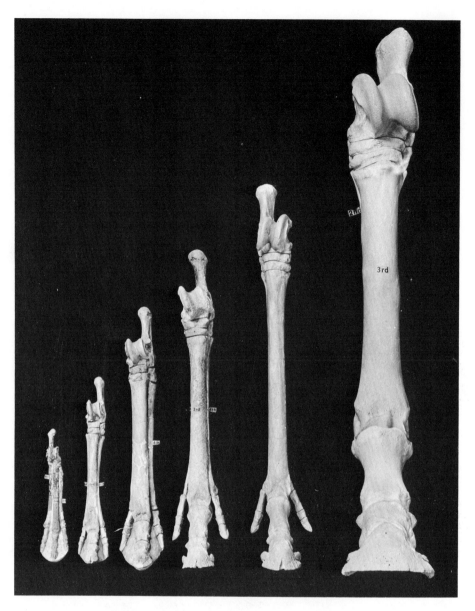

Eohippus to Equus; from five toes to a single hoof

As he had grown taller, his head and neck had lengthened, too. He was not a browser any more; he became a grass-eater. His molar teeth developed high crowns and a good cement covering for grinding the coarse grasses that were gritty with dust and sand.

Scientists call him *Merychippus*, the first of the grazers.

10

Pliohippus, the One-Toed Grazer

In the long, long history of the next ten million years, mountains continued to rise, the climate became cooler, and the horse continued to adapt to the earth's changes. Gradually he attained the height of a donkey and he grew a bristly broom-tail like a donkey and his mane was stiff and upright.

But the biggest change was in his feet. No longer was he three-toed. The middle toe had grown blunt and broad and stronger than the others. In fact, he walked on his middle toenail, which had thickened considerably. The

Pliohippus, the one-toed grazer

PLIOHIPPUS
Mother and Colt of Fossil Ancestral
Horse of Nebraska. Modeled by A. C.
Simons, after skeleton in the Hall of
the Age of Mammals

other toes slowly disappeared; only slivers of bone, known as splints, were reminders of the lost toes. Now he was powerfully adapted to gallop over the hard-packed earth.

Along with these changes his head and neck lengthened even more and his eyes were set even wider apart. This gave him excellent vision. He could see behind as well as ahead! In the vastness of the plains he could sight faraway enemies in any direction. He was well fitted to live in his wide grassy world. His name, *Pliohippus,* means "more recent horse."

Equus, the True Horse

Equus, the horse of today, is bigger and stronger in every way than Pliohippus, his "great-great-grandfather." His legs

Equus Scotti, an early horse about the size of a small mustang

are longer, his middle toe has terminated in a stout hoof, his head is much larger, his eyes are still farther back and they have even greater scope. The gap behind his front teeth has grown large enough now to hold a bit. And the teeth themselves are marvels of efficiency. Unlike human teeth, his molars are very high-crowned and they keep on growing until the horse is old. As the surface is gradually worn away by grinding, they sharpen themselves! The softer cement wears down, the ridges of hard enamel protrude and keep the surface rough for more and more grinding.

Between Eohippus, the dawn horse, and Equus, the true horse, there were fifty million years of changes—big and little, rapid and slow. And most of the story happened right here on this continent.

Zebras graze on the floor of a crater in southeast Africa

1

Men hunted the horse long before they tamed him. They made magic drawings of him to help them. These paintings were done on the walls of a cave in Lascaux, France, over 20,000 years ago.

2

French Embassy Press and Information Division

3

4

Domestic horses soon spread everywhere. The long-necked steed at
left, with his Iron Age rider, is from Cyprus while the horse-shaped
cheekpiece above came from ancient Persia. The bronze horse below,
pulling a sacred sun-disc, was made in Denmark about 1,100 B.C.

The Metropolitan Museum of Art, Rogers Fund, 1923

6

Horses were brought to Egypt by foreign conquerors. The Egyptians, fighting in light chariots like the one below, drove them out again—with the help of horses. Egyptian artists mastered the horse in another way, as the delightfully natural sketch above shows.

7

Magnum

The nobleman of the Middle Ages ruled because he was mounted. His great war horse carried him quickly and easily, even in full armor. He learned to ride almost as soon as he could walk. Even in peacetime, he lived in the saddle, although he gave up his war horse for a lighter mount called a palfrey. This was the horse that his lady also rode (right). He rarely walked anywhere, and even went hawking on horseback (above). And a poor knight who had only one horse used it to work his fields when he was not fighting. It was said—and with some truth—that the knights prized their horses only slightly less than their hounds and far above their wives.

10

Pierpont Morgan Library

For centuries, the horse was the king of the battlefield. During the Middle Ages, most battles were decided by mounted knights. Even when guns brought an end to the age of knights, horses still had a part to play. They hauled the guns. And cavalry were the crack troops in every army. The horse also became the mark of an officer, as it had once been the mark of a nobleman. An officer had to be able to ride, and some were not only good horsemen but good officers too. George Washington (left) was not only one of the great generals of his day but was highly respected for his skill in the saddle. Through all his campaigns, his constant companion was his sorrel, Nelson.

On deposit at Museum of Fine Arts, Boston

In the fifteenth century, the city-states of Italy hired professional soldiers to do their fighting. The condottieri, as they were called, fought for pay, not for glory. They needed faster, lighter horses than the knights' chargers to carry them out of danger as quickly as possible. They had a high regard for the safety of their skins, because they knew that they could not collect their pay if they were killed. So for a time war became much tamer than it had been. Even so, several condottieri made their marks as soldiers. One of the most famous was Guidoriccio da Fogliano (above), general of Siena.

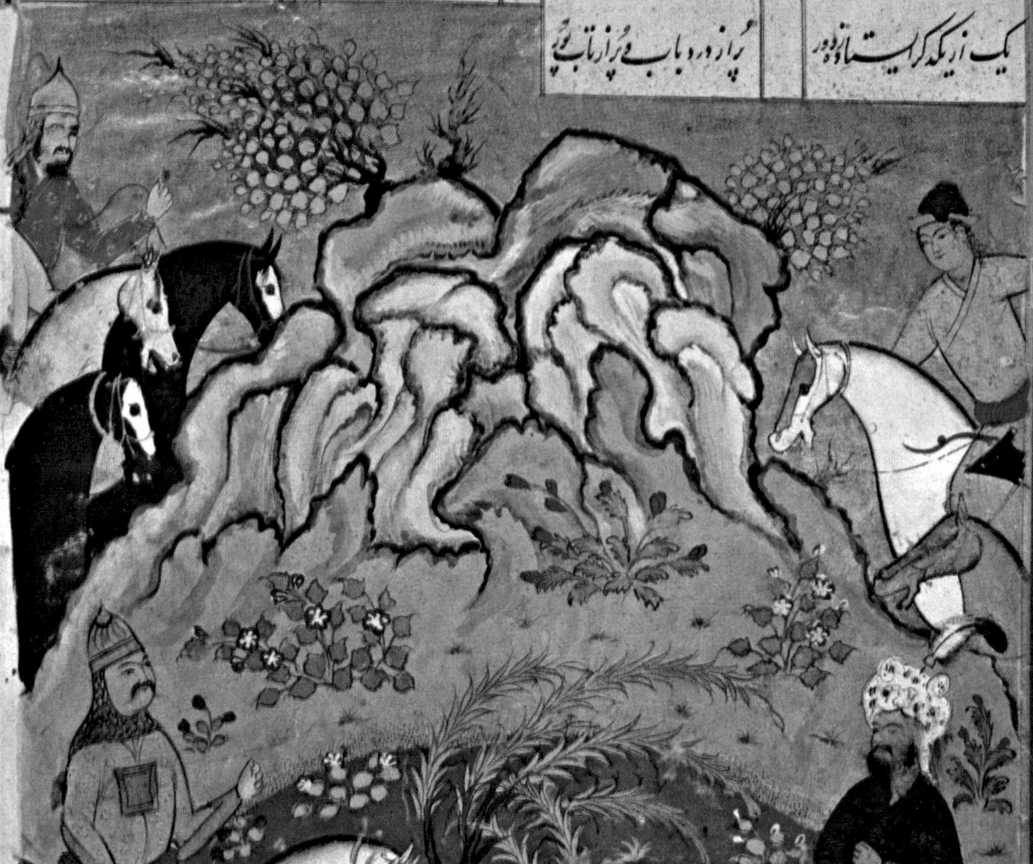

Every country has a favorite horse story. Persia's is the tale of the great hero Rustem (opposite), his bay Ruksh "whose renown was noised through all the earth" and his son Sohrab, whom he killed by mistake. England's is the story of highwayman Dick Turpin (right), who rode his Black Bess nearly 200 miles in a day to avoid capture. Greece has the legend of the wooden horse of Troy, a great favorite in the Middle Ages when the enamel plaque below was made.

In the 20th century, cars, planes and trains have taken the horse's place. But before that, nothing would have moved without him. He pulled the plow and the barge. He hauled fire engines (opposite at top) and carried the mail—the Pony Express (right) could take a letter from St. Joseph, Missouri, to San Francisco in less than ten days. He even created traffic jams. The painting opposite at bottom shows Trafalgar Square in London in the early 1800's—a tangle of carts, carriages, riders and, on the left, a horse-drawn stage, the forerunner of today's buses. Horses were also a part of man's pastimes. Today, we can still enjoy a sleigh ride through the snow as the 19th-century couple below are doing. And there is one kind of horse that everyone can ride today. He is on the next page.

Pony Express History and Art Gallery, Sao Rafael, California

The Wild Relatives of the Horse

Today there are a few horses still roaming the world who are closely related to those prehistoric horses. When Stone Age man first captured the early ones, there were some that refused to bow to his will. They went their own way, an independent and wild way, and in the long years developed into other branches of the horse family.

Today they include several species which are horselike, but are not the same as the horses we know. They are the wild relatives, real live relics of prehistoric times.

The One and Only Wild Horse

Almost every day on television and radio we can tune in

on "westerns." The hero is usually a hard-riding cowboy who rounds up a band of untamed horses, captures one of the wildest, breaks him, and gallops off into the sunset. We sigh with envy and go to bed dreaming of the herds of wild horses just waiting to be captured. But they are not really wild horses. They are *feral* horses, which means that they or their ancestors were once broken to be ridden or driven. Later they managed to escape and went wild.

But here we are talking about truly wild horses, the only horses that have never been tamed by man. The one most closely resembling our own horse is the Przewalski of the great Gobi desert of Asia. He stands about the size of a stunted horse. His coat is rough and its color is a dull dark yellow, lighter on the sides than on the back, and almost cream-colored on the belly.

This Asiatic horse is not only wild but woolly. In winter his coat grows long and shaggy, his mane is bristly as a broom, and on either side of his face he bushes out with whiskers. Toward summer these whiskers disappear and he grows a goatee instead.

The Gobi desert where he lives is fierce, rugged country. A fiery sun bakes the sands by day and biting winds blow at night. The seasons change sharply from burning summer to icy winter. Animals and people both have adapted to these extremes. The wandering tribes who roam the desert are built squatty like the horses. Their hair, too, is coarse and thick. And in winter they wear shaggy furs, and even long tails on their caps.

Being a nomadic people they wanted to break the wild horses and use them as pack animals. But they never succeeded. Again and again they tried. They even captured

Przewalski's horse is the only true wild horse today

the tiny foals and raised them in captivity, but the wildness persisted. Always they escaped to be free again.

These tameless horses were given their curious name because of a Russian explorer, Colonel Nikolai Przewalski, who was the first man to make a report on them. He brought back a skull and a skin, and told about the scraggly beasts and that they had developed a tribal cunning far greater than tame horses.

Their life, he wrote, had a set pattern. They dozed in the heat of the day and traveled by night to watering

17

places and to cool upland meadows. They marched in a long parade, the leader in front, the others following Indian file over the same path which their ancestors had beaten down through the years. At all times, even when they were grazing peacefully or sleeping, a scout kept watch to warn of enemies. When one approached, he bugled the alarm and the horses grouped quickly into a bunch, the weaklings in the center, the fighters on the outside, ready to flail out with their hard, flinty hoofs.

Our wild-animal zoos are helping to preserve the Przewalski horse. If you would like to see what he looks like, you could visit the Brookfield Zoo in Chicago, the Zoological Gardens in New York, the National Zoological Park in Washington, D. C., or the Catskill Game Farm at Catskill, New York.

The Onagers

The onager is another wild relative of the horse. In Bible times he was known as the wild ass, and the Old Testament gives a good account of his lonely life: "He scorneth the multitude of the city . . . The range of the mountains is his pasture, and he searcheth after every green thing."

The onager is a much handsomer animal than the Przewalski; sleeker of coat, cleaner of head, and finer of limb. His ears are bigger, almost mule-size, and his tail is tufted. However, he is not a cross between a donkey and a horse, but is his own distinct breed. His coloring, a grayish white, is so very faint that he is almost invisible against the desert sands.

18

The onager, another wild relative, is becoming extinct

The Persians think onager meat a great delicacy, and to-day they still hunt the few of these animals that are left. Because of his extreme speed, hunters consider an onager chase great sport. In fact, they often use relays of horses to catch him!

This small horse-relative once ranged the earth all through central Asia and India and westward to Palestine. But he is fast becoming extinct. Soon, it is feared, none will remain to be a symbol of the wild freedom of ancient days.

Luckily there are still a few onagers in zoos—at Lincoln Park in Chicago, at Fairmount Park in Philadelphia, and a whole colony of them at the Catskill Game Farm in Catskill, New York.

The Wild Ass

Another member of the wild species is the mouse-colored true wild ass, the direct ancestor of today's donkeys. He can be found only in northeastern Africa, where he lives in small herds, scrounging for a living in the low stony hills. Yet in spite of his skimpy fare and harsh life he is a strong, fleet, round-bellied fellow.

Wild asses

He has the same wistful appeal as the donkeys we see in our own country—the enormous ears, the white circle around his almond-shaped eyes, the soft white muzzle, the tufty tail; and, of course, he brays like a steam whistle. When he runs, he scarcely bends his knees. It looks as if he had pogo sticks for legs. All of these characteristics he has passed on to our donkeys of today.

Zebras

The zebra is the striped relative of the horse, who is still running wild and free in Africa. Because his flesh and hide both are valuable, he is often hunted by the natives. And if he escapes them, he still must outrun the jackals and lions, hyenas and panthers.

He would probably now be extinct if it were not for his stripes, which make a good camouflage. He blends so well with the tall grasses and the slim-trunked trees that in the distance you and I might not even see him. But if we are lucky enough to have a close-up view, we are dazzled by the stunning pattern of his stripes. They may be vertical or horizontal or oblique; and some are wide, some narrow; some are black, some brown. A few zebras even have stripes in their manes.

Zebras are first cousins of the horse, and some naturalists believe that little Eohippus may have been a striped creature. One famous scientist, George Gaylord Simpson, says, "Instead of thinking of zebras as striped horses, perhaps we should think of horses as stripeless zebras!"

An unknown Egyptian carved this horse more than 3000 years ago

Man and Horse Together

For untold years the wild horse lived tameless and free, traveling in bands, seeking grazing grounds and water holes. Early man-creatures lived in small groups, too, wandering much as horses did in search of food and water. They were flesh-eaters, however, instead of grass-eaters, and they hunted wild game, including the horse. They had no thought of putting him to work. Dogs were their draft animals.

Of course, we know that horse and man did get together, but how or when is still a question. It was long before man could write and historians have had to reason out how it happened.

Perhaps, they say, a boy of the Stone Age came upon a deserted wild colt, too weak to keep up with the herd. If

A wild horse hunt, from an Assyrian wall-carving

the boy's father had been on hand, he might have killed it
to provide meat for his family. But suppose he was off
hunting bison and bears; and by the time he returned, the
Stone Age boy was feeding goat's milk to the colt, and
they had become friends.

As the days passed and the colt grew strong, the boy began comparing him to his dog. If the dog could pull little
loads, why couldn't the colt pull big ones? We can imagine
the boy urging his new pet to drag heavier and heavier
baskets of stones until at last the father saw what a help
this "big dog" could be.

Where did this drama take place? It probably occurred

many, many times in different ways in different places in the Old World—that vast area which is now Europe, Africa, and Asia.

When did it take place? It must have been before 2500 B.C., for we know that by then invaders and wandering nomads had brought the tamed horse to all the civilized areas of the world. Man and horse were working together.

When we speak of early civilization, we think of peaceful people—plowing and planting and making pottery. But the truth is that they were far more interested in conquest and war. Here the horse was vital.

One of the best histories of that early time is the Bible, and in the Old Testament there is frequent mention of war horses. Job vividly described a horse in battle: "The glory of his nostrils is terrible. He paweth in the valley, and rejoiceth in his strength. He goeth on to meet the armed men. He swalloweth the ground with fierceness and rage."

Before the coming of the horse, ancient peoples used donkeys

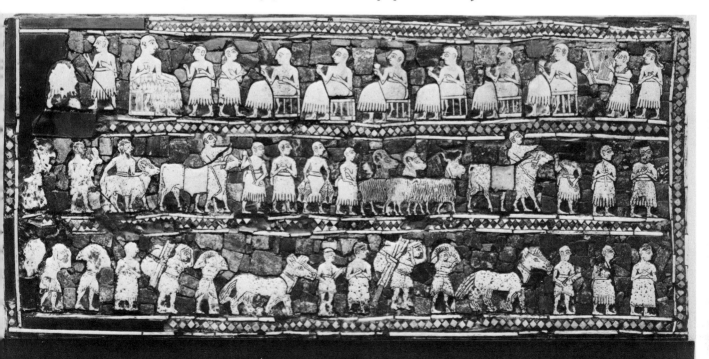

A head from the Parthenon

And Jeremiah proclaimed that the Lord said: "The snorting of his horses was heard; the whole land trembled at the sound of the neighing of his strong ones. For they are come, and have devoured the land, and all that is in it." And in the book of Habakkuk the horses of the Chaldeans are described as "swifter than leopards, more fierce than evening wolves."

The early Greeks, too, were proud of their war horses, but they prized them far more for their beauty. They were skilled artists and used the horse as a model for statues in marble and bronze, and they painted his likeness on enormous vases. Today people from all over the world visit the

26

Parthenon in Athens and there they stand in awe before the carvings in relief of spirited horses and their young bareback riders.

The Greeks were the first people to use the horse in sport. Today's famous Olympics stem from their ancient contests held on the plains of Olympia. The most exciting event of all was the four-horse chariot race. Often it turned into a bloody battle, which the athletes considered splendid training for war.

In every country battles were being fought by warriors standing erect in open chariots. Each one was drawn by teams of two, three and even four horses. The chariots were painted gold and were beautiful to look upon, but they were lightweight and fragile. Scythelike blades of metal were mounted on the axles, and when chariots collided, horses were slashed, men were pitched overboard, and the beautiful golden chariots were reduced to kindling wood.

A better way of fighting had to be found. Riding into battle on horseback was the answer.

A modern nomad and his spirited Arabian

Riding Into Battle

Without the aid of his horses the Arabian prophet, Mohammed, could never have built one of the biggest empires on earth. He linked not only horse and rider, but also horse and religion.

As a young man he was in the habit of going up into the mountains to pray, and one day he came down in great excitement. The angel Gabriel, he said, had appeared in a vision and commanded him: "Arise and preach! Magnify the Lord." Mohammed fully believed that he had been chosen the true prophet of Allah and that his people must carry the message of one god to the whole world.

His tribesmen seized on the idea. They had always lived for, with, and on their horses—shared their tents with them, raced them across the desert, and fought bareback in little skirmishes. Now they had a big goal. They must save all the peoples of the world. Their battle cry was: "Accept Allah! Pay tribute or die!"

Fired with the same zeal as their leader, they set out to conquer the world. First they swooped down on their neighbors, the Syrians. When they were converted the two forces joined and together they swept on, overpowering the Nubians, the Egyptians, the Berbers, the Moors, until all of these nomadic people were united through religion and way of life.

As Mohammed swallowed up tribe after tribe, he taught them his own rules of horsemanship: never to thrash a horse, never to tie him by the neck, but always to tether him by a hind leg. In his religion man and horse were destined to be constant companions. "Every grain of barley given to a horse," he said, "is entered by God in the Register of Good Works."

As his military and religious crusade gained in strength,

his empire grew. It spread ever westward in the shape of a big half moon around the Mediterranean Sea. At last the fighting hordes reached the northernmost tip of the African continent. Here they were stopped by the sea.

Ahead lay the deep blue waters and, in the distance beyond, the green wooded hills of Spain. After the miles of parched desert behind them, the greenness beckoned invitingly. Besides, word had come that civil war was raging in Spain and the people might be ripe for conquest.

An advance guard of Moors crossed the narrow strait of water. They stole some Spanish boats and sailed back. Then they loaded their mounts aboard and scudded across to Spain. The rumors had been true, for the Spaniards put up only small resistance. The Moors returned with the good news. In the months that followed, more and more tribes made the crossing.

Meanwhile the Spaniards were preparing to fight back, and soon they became superior. Their swords and daggers were more deadly than the thin lances of the Moslems. Their horses were larger and stronger, and man and horse both were shielded by heavy armor.

But as the invaders kept on coming, the big Spanish horses were outnumbered and outmaneuvered by the little Arab and Barb horses. They could dart like lightning around and between the armored beasts. Besides, the Moslems had developed great skill with their lances, unhorsing their enemies if they could not penetrate the joints of their armor. And so Spain, too, was added to Mohammed's growing empire.

Filled with triumph by their successes, the Moslems next swept into France, hoping to go on and conquer the whole of Europe. But they were abruptly stopped by Charles the Hammer in a bloody battle near the city of Tours. By now Mohammed was dead, and the new Moslem leaders were no match for this army of mighty warriors known as Franks. Their mounts were Flemish horses, big and black and powerful, and their number was legion. When they charged into the delicate Arabian horses, it was as if a battery of caterpillar tractors had plowed head-on into a fleet of little race cars. In the big Battle of Tours in the year 732, the Moslem march into Europe was finally stopped.

Even though the crusade into France was a failure, Moslem rule in Spain lasted for hundreds of years. The Spaniards never really merged with their conquerors, but they did acquire new ideas of horsemanship. For one thing they learned an entirely different way of riding. The old Spanish style was known as *a la brida*. Long stirrup leathers were used so that the rider's legs were straight, his knees unbent. His saddle was like a chair, fitting closely about the hips, holding him stiff and upright. As he often wore armor, he was unable to twist and turn. And so, riding *a la brida,* while dignified and picturesque, was not practical in war.

The Mohammedans, on the other hand, rode much like our jockeys of today with very short stirrups, or none at all. And they sat with their weight well forward, saving the horse's back. The Spaniards called this type of riding *a la jineta,* after one of the conquering Berber tribes known as Zenetes. It soon became a mark of distinction for a Spanish gentleman to be able to ride either way, *a la brida* or *a la jineta*. On the tombstones of the Spanish caballeros

A la brida   *A la jineta*

these words often appeared: "Here lies Don Juan, who
rode well in both styles."

The Spaniards learned something even more important
from their conquerors. They learned how to breed finer
horses. By crossing their own stock with the swift little
Arabians and Barbs, they produced a new breed called
jennets, from the new style of riding. These jennets were
neither as big as the Spanish horses nor as small as the
Orientals. They were sturdy, stout, and strong. In fact,
they were so hardy that Spain became the envy of all Europe for the quality of its horses.

And so the Mohammedans not only introduced a new
religion but helped to found a new breed of horse and to
raise Spain in importance in the eyes of Europe.

33

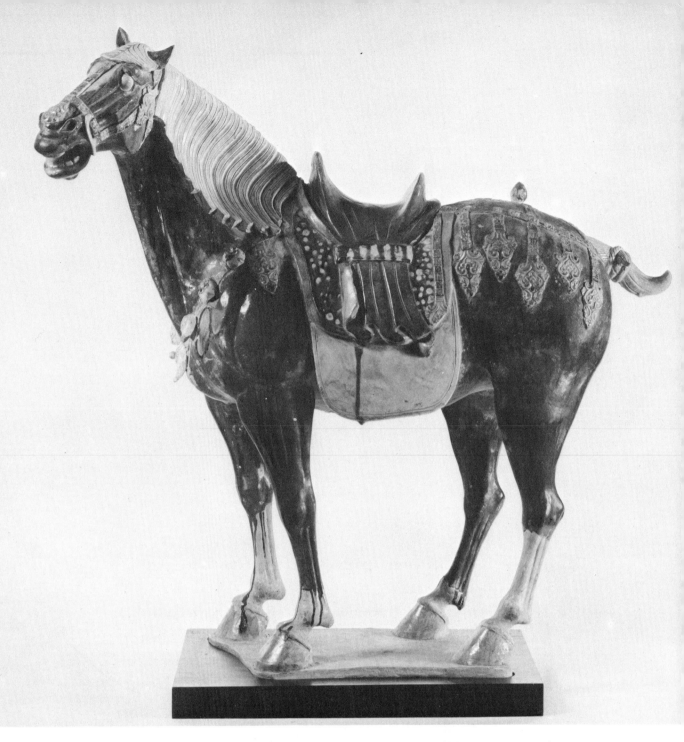

The Mongol's pony must have looked like this one, made by a Chinese potter centuries before Genghis Khan was born.

5

The Horsemen From Hell

Empires are born and die, and no matter how cruel and bloodthirsty their conquests, something that is good nearly always lives on. This was true of the Mohammedan Empire. Before it collapsed, the worship of idols had been abolished and a one-god religion adopted by multitudes of people. The great prophet had taught many fine principles —the brotherhood of man, the wisdom of obeying the ten commandments, and also the art of horse care and riding.

Several hundred years later another great empire was born—this time in Asia. The leader was a fierce Mongol warrior named Genghis Khan. At the age of thirteen he was already a chieftain, and when he became man-grown, he too had a vision. He claimed that the "Eternal Blue Sky" had chosen him to conquer and command the world.

To the Mongols the sky was their god, and so they bowed to this confident young ruler and accepted his leadership.

By the time Genghis Khan was thirty, he had built an army 700,000 strong, and like Mohammed he set out to conquer the world. He and his soldiers pillaged and plundered and burned cities and slaughtered people by the millions. They were known as the Horsemen From Hell. No one seemed able to stop them. They swept over the land, seizing nearly all of China, Persia, India, Turkestan, and even a big slice of Russia.

Like Mohammed, too, Genghis Khan was a splendid horseman. He saw to it that every male member of his forty tribes was mounted and had a spare horse besides. Before every campaign he organized training camps where he taught the skills of war, and that mobility was more important than sheer strength. His military tactics were so clever they are often used in today's machine-age wars.

Under his direction the Mongols developed a light speedy horse which they valued above human life. It was not only quick transportation, but a shield and a weapon in war. And in the last extreme it was food—dead or alive. Soldiers suffering from thirst drank mare's milk, and in great emergency they were known to slit a horse's veins, drink the blood, and, when they had staunched the bleeding, mount and ride off again.

Genghis Khan really had two gods—the Eternal Blue Sky and his horses. Though ruthless to people, he was kind to horses. Before crossing the vast Gobi desert he waited for spring so that there would be fresh grazing. And he never used horses to pull loads; asses and camels were good enough for that. Even slave help was preferred in order to save horses for war. And woe to a horse thief! When caught, he had to pay ten for one, or sacrifice his sons and daughters or his own life.

Never satisfied with his victories, Genghis Khan went on invading and killing until his empire became the largest in the world, stretching all the way across Asia and even into Europe.

Finally it grew so big it began to topple of its own weight, like toy blocks piled too high. The collapse came when the Horsemen From Hell were on the very brink of their goal. It was one thing to thunder across the world on horseback, crushing everything before them, but quite another to hold onto the lands and govern them. As long as the Mongols were on their horses, it seemed they were unconquerable. But once they dismounted and tried to rule the world on foot, they failed.

Yet in spite of the savagery and the ruthlessness of the Mongol conquest, again some good was accomplished. Roads were built between Europe and Asia, and peoples of different cultures met each other and began to trade goods and knowledge. Oriental delicacies in foods and also fine fabrics were introduced. The Chinese arts of the porcelain makers, the lacquer workers, the jade carvers, the silk growers and weavers, the paper makers, the stencil printers were shared with the West.

As for the fiery steeds of the Mongols, they were distributed over most of the civilized world. They had come through the ordeals of war tougher, stronger, hardier—like steel tempered by fire.

The First of His Race

6

The Horse Crosses the Atlantic

Before it reached Italy or Spain, the empire of Genghis Khan had crumbled. But news of the conquests had turned men's thoughts more and more to the untold treasures of the Orient. Christopher Columbus was one of those who longed to find a direct route to that fabulous, faraway land. He already knew that the world was round, so he set out to find a way to go east by sailing west! This would be far easier than the long march over desert wastes and craggy mountains.

Of course we know that instead of reaching the Orient, Columbus discovered our continent. Here he found no rich fabrics or spices. But what concerns us is that he found no horses whatever! None at all. Where had they gone?

We remember that little Eohippus, the Dawn Horse, and

even Equus had once roamed in great herds over the grasslands of our western plains. Many, many skeletons have been uncovered to prove it. But what happened to all of the horses?

No one really knows; the answer is locked in the secrets of the past. We can only piece together bits of knowledge gathered by students of the earth and its creatures.

Ages ago, they say, when the earth was warmer there was a land bridge between what is now Alaska and Russia, and many of the horses of our continent trekked across that bridge. Why did they leave? Perhaps they were forced to find new pastures because of the great hordes of incoming bison, who were competitors for their grasslands. Or it may have been drought or change of climate that ruined the grazing grounds. Whatever the reason, many horses migrated to Asia. Later the bridge of land disappeared into the sea, and they could never get back.

What happened to the horses that did not migrate? We know that they all died out. They may have been weakened by hunger or disease and then devoured by jaguars or mountain lions. Some scientists even suggest that man was their worst enemy, for he killed and ate them.

No one really knows. But the fact remains that when the Spanish explorers discovered America in 1492, there was not a living horse on the continent.

The First Arrivals

It was Don Hernando Cortés who first brought horses back to America. He was a daring adventurer with fiery black eyes and shining black mustachios. The King of Spain ordered him to conquer, colonize, and Christianize the New World. In the year 1518 he went first to the island of Cuba and there he spent a whole year organizing his expedition of men and horses and supplies. Then he set sail and landed on the spot where the city of Vera Cruz now stands.

It took nineteen days to sail just the distance from Cuba to Mexico. The ocean sea, as they called it, had been choppy, the food scarce, and most of the soldiers were seasick and homesick. After unloading the horses and supplies, the first thing Cortés did was to burn the ships right there on the beach so that his men could not return home.

Among his soldiers was Bernal Díaz, a young man of sharp eye and memory. He kept a diary of the whole expedition, and we have him to thank for giving us a record of the first horses to set foot on our western hemisphere in thousands of years. He wrote:

"The horses were divided up among the ships and loaded, mangers erected, and a store of corn and hay put on board. I will now list the mares and horses:
1. a dark chestnut stallion belonging to Captain Cortés.
2. a very good sorrel mare, excellent for tilting and for racing.
3. a swift gray mare.
4. a sturdy gray mare which we called La Rabona (bobtailed), fast and well broken.
5. a dark brown horse that was quite satisfactory.
6. a parched sorrel, useless for war.

7. a dark bay stallion, fast and well reined.
8. a light bay horse with three white stockings, not very good.
9. a barren gray mare, a pacer which seldom galloped.
10. a dark brown horse, good, and a grand runner.
11. a good chestnut horse, a beautiful color, ran very well.
12. a pinto with white stockings, well reined.
13. a dark roan with white patches, turned out worthless.
14. a very good bay, an excellent runner.
15. a black horse called 'El arriero,' probably leader of a pack train, one of the best horses in the fleet.
16. a brown mare that foaled on board ship."

Legend has it that the brown mare died soon after landing and her little colt escaped to the wilds, where he was mothered by a doe. He was never tamed by man and lived free all his life.

Although Cortés and his men had been sent to Mexico to conquer and Christianize, they were really greedy for gold. They had heard exciting rumors that the native Aztec Indians waded in gold up to their knees. Of course this was an exaggeration, but the Aztecs were indeed a mighty race. They mined for gold and silver and precious stones, and their temples and palaces were piled high with treasure.

At first they were friendly to Cortés. Their emperor, Montezuma, presented him with breastplates of gold, studded with gems, and an alligator's head made of solid gold and a great golden wheel. But soon the Emperor realized that

Xaltelolco.

Cortés' horses were the key to his conquest of Mexico

the Spaniards had come as warriors, not friends.

The battles that followed were curiously one-sided. Although there were thousands of Indians for every Spaniard, the Spaniards won. The Indians used only slingstones and arrows, while the Spaniards had guns and ammunition. But, far more important, they had horses. The Indians had never seen any before and they fled in terror at the very sight of

43

the charging beasts. They thought horse and man were all one fierce, superhuman monster that would eat them alive.

When the Spaniards conquered the Aztec nation, the scribe of the expedition, Bernal Díaz, wrote in his diary: "In the unrelenting fight of one against thousands, the horses were our fortress . . . our only hope of survival." And Cortés himself sent word back to Spain: "Next to God, we owed our victory to the horses."

Two Hundred and Fifty Horses

Stories of the great riches to be found in the New World excited the King of Spain. Let's have more expeditions, he thought. Next he chose Hernando De Soto, a successful explorer who had already taken part in the conquest of Peru. The King commanded him to go out in search of the fabled city of El Dorado, which was supposed to be built of solid gold.

De Soto, like Cortés, made careful preparation. In Cuba he bought up all of the finest horses that had been brought from Spain or bred on the island, and then he set sail. With several hundred men and two hundred and fifty horses he landed in what is now Tampa Bay, Florida. Of course he never found the golden city of El Dorado, but for years he searched, marching ever westward into vast uncharted territory. At last he reached the Mississippi River, probably the first white man ever to see it.

He managed to cross the wide muddy waters, his men poling over on crude rafts, their horses swimming alongside. The Indians watching on the banks were awed by the big animals that could swim. And they looked upon De Soto as a powerful god who could turn beasts into fish. Soon after crossing the river, De Soto -fell sick and died. To hide the fact that he was only mortal, his men buried him in the dark of night in the rushing waters of the Mississippi. The Indians were told that the great white god had been called home to the sun.

Fifteen Hundred Strong

In spite of De Soto's failure, the rumors of gold kept growing. Now there was talk of greater wealth even than El Dorado. Men spoke of "The Seven Cities of Cibola" whose streets were paved with gold and studded with emeralds.

Soon a third Spanish explorer set forth on a third expedition. He was Francisco Coronado, and his army was by far the largest and most impressive. He mustered three hundred men and fifteen hundred horses and set out for the unknown lands beyond the great river of De Soto. There, at the tail end of the world, in what is now New Mexico, he sought the seven golden cities of Cibola. Imagine his disappointment when instead of the seven rich cities he found seven little Indian villages of the Zuñi tribe. And their only treasure was the modest turquoise instead of costly emeralds.

Each of the villages was built as a large apartment house, forming walled terraces of brick around a central plaza. The Spanish conquest might well have been stopped by these strange fortresses, and also by the greater number of Zuñis, but again horses turned the tide. The Indians were terrified of them. In superstitious fear they allowed themselves to be conquered. And again the report went back to Spain, "Next to God, we owe our victory to the horses."

The Horse Indians

We know, of course, that the conquered Indians eventually became expert riders—even more skilled than their conquerors. They threw away the saddle, leaped aboard the horse bareback, and locked both legs about his barrel. Then, twisting their bodies, they could shoot their arrows from any angle, even from underneath a horse's neck.

How humiliating to the Spanish warrior! Just as he aimed his gun at an Indian's head, the head suddenly vanished, to be shielded by the horse itself.

This skill and daring did not come about overnight. First the Indians had to obtain horses. And even before that, they had to overcome their terror of them. This must have happened in battle when Indian braves discovered that an arrow could kill either a rider *or* his horse. And so they realized

47

that man and horse were not one monster after all; they broke apart into two beings. Now the Indians knew the horse was mortal. Anyone could ride him—red man or white!

Runaways?

How the Indians captured their horses is still the subject of sharp debate. Some historians think they simply lassoed strays from the Spanish expeditions, and an exciting fable has been built around this belief. It starts out with a powerful stallion bolting away from the explorers and tearing like lightning across the plains. As he flees, he bugles to the mares to follow and a few of the more adventurous heed his call. In due time they have colts and grand-colts and great-grand-colts and great-great-grand-colts until the plains are simply alive with horses.

The facts, however, are even more exciting than the legend. But first we must explode the theory of the runaways. Cortés, you remember, brought over sixteen horses and only five were mares; and most of them were slain in battle. Twenty years later De Soto brought two hundred and fifty horses. Of this number several died on the voyage, one hundred and fifty in battle, and the rest were eaten to keep the men alive. As for Coronado's army of horses, they perished in combat, in hailstorms and in buffalo fights.

We feel sure of these facts and figures because horses were so valuable to the early explorers that each one's death was carefully recorded. Human losses, on the contrary, were too numerous to write down. Cortés admitted that he valued one horse as twenty men. De Soto and Coronado felt the same way. They, too, kept precise records, whether an animal was killed in battle or by wild animals or poisonous weeds. And in all of this accounting there is no mention of runaways.

But even supposing a few horses had escaped, could they have survived their enemies—wolves traveling in packs, savage mountain lions, and deadly rattlesnakes? More unlikely still, could they have survived the Indians? On the rare occasions when the Indians did capture a few horses, they had but one thought. Here was food. And so they would drive them over a cliff into a gulch and slaughter them. Horse meat, they discovered, was as good as buffalo meat.

But if the early Indians actually hunted and ate horses, how did they ever become expert riders?

It was the Spanish missionaries who changed their ways. They had come to convert the Indians, and it was their hope to replace the bow and arrow with the saw and the plow. So they established small settlements where the natives were welcomed and invited to work and worship.

The Indians became expert riders and invented a form of polo

FREDERIC REMINGTON —

The Indians were attracted to the quiet, black-cloaked monks who carried Bibles and crosses instead of guns. From them they learned peaceful pursuits—farming and sheep herding and the use of horses as beasts of burden. But what intrigued them most was that the white man had no special power over the horse; he behaved the same for the red man as for the white. By example and teaching the Indian realized that horses were strong and wonderful workers. They could pull twice their weight. And with a man on their back they could skim across the plains as fast as the wind.

The settlers who followed the missionaries set up large ranches for raising livestock and they used the Indians as servants. But when the ranchers discovered how quickly and easily the Indians could handle horses, they sternly forbade them to ride. This was a privilege only for the Spanish gentlemen.

Horse Thieves!

Silently, grimly, the Indians bided their time. In secret they watched their masters—observed carefully how to mount, how to guide a horse to right or left, how to spur it into a gallop. By now all of their early fears were gone. They saw in the horse a strong and willing partner. He could drag their belongings from winter to summer quarters. He could chase the buffalo. He could carry them in battle.

Because the horse was denied to them, he became all the more desirable. The only way to secure one, they concluded, was by rustling. And so horse-stealing became a sport, a daring and dangerous sport.

Once an Indian made up his mind which horse he wanted, it was only a matter of time. Waiting was the trick. Waiting days or weeks for the moon to wane, waiting minutes or hours for a wind to blow his scent away, waiting for sounds within the ranch buildings to be quieted by sleep.

Then with eyes sharp as a cat's, on silent soft-moccasined feet he crept toward the corral, squeezed through the fence rails, crawled up to his prize, talking in the low guttural tones the horse already knew. Gently he looped a riata around the prized one's neck and led him, willingly, from the corral. Once out of earshot, he leaped aboard and went galloping toward his own camp, whooping for joy.

Soon these forays grew in numbers and daring. The Indians did not stop with an occasional theft. Horses were carried off by the tens and twenties. All the way from Mexico to Canada raiding parties made life unsafe for the settlers. Even bullets were of little avail. While the white man was loading his gun to discharge one blast, the Indian could swivel around on his horse's back and shoot a dozen arrows!

The tide was turning with swift violence. Yesterday the Spaniards had overpowered the Indians. Now the Indians were halting the Spaniards and making off with their dearest possessions—*horses*.

Mustangs. Cowboys still round up the descendents of Cortés' horses

Horse Trading and Raiding

Stealing horses from the Spaniards was but half the fun for the Indians. Soon they began horse-lifting from each other under the guise of trading. In exchange for a few head of horses a horseless tribe would offer blankets and beans, maize and moccasins enough to last a whole year. The trade completed, the new horsemen would sneak up on the other tribe under cover of darkness and lure away more horses. Sometimes they even took back their blankets and beans and maize and moccasins.

Each Indian nation tried to outsmart the other. At one time the Blackfeet stole 1200 horses from the Crows and the Crows immediately turned about and stole 2000 from the Blackfeet, who in turn took 3000 from the Crows.

Every tribe believed implicitly that the Good Spirit had

created the horse especially for them. Of course, one had only to note the Spanish brands on the horses' flanks to know where they had come from. But such details never concerned the Indians; they just decorated their horses with eagle feathers, daubed them with war paint, and off they rode with only a rope for a bridle and a blanket for a saddle—or none at all.

The Birth of the Mustang

The Indian braves were expert riders, but they paid no attention to the care of their horses. It was the Indian squaw who had to water and feed them. And in winter they were left to forage for themselves, pawing beneath the snow for matted leaves and dried grasses.

Nor did the Indians pay any attention to horse breeding. Of all the tribes only the Nez Percé of the Pacific Northwest showed an interest in keeping their breed of horse pure. They had their own spotted Appaloosas, and they prized them so highly that they bred only the best to the best. All the other tribes were more interested in numbers than in quality. In their eyes a tribe was rich and famous according to how many horses it owned. There was no thought whatever for the future. The plains were an endless sea of grass with pasture aplenty for all the horses yet to be born.

As a result, the Indian ponies increased in numbers until there were perhaps two million of them ranging the plains from Texas to Oregon. They were called mustangs, from the Spanish word *mesteño*, meaning a grazer, strayed or wild. This lack of selection in breeding, while it produced a scrubby-looking beast, could never extinguish the fire and spirit of the Arab-Barb blood. In fact, sometimes the scrubbier a mustang looked, the more rugged he seemed to be.

The Buffalo Runners

Their wealth of horses brought to the Indians a new kind of freedom. In the old days a buffalo hunt had been dusty, sweaty, grueling work. On foot, the hunters would stampede a whole herd, driving them into a narrow ravine. There they

set fire to the grass, making death slow and horrible. It was wholesale slaughter. It had to be, or the Indians themselves would have been trampled to death.

But in a mustang the Indian owned a skilled buffalo runner. Now he could race neck and neck with one of the big beasts, and by gripping his mount solidly with his legs, he kept his hands free to shoot an arrow and fell his quarry on the spot. At last he could kill buffalo one at a time, as he needed them.

With his new-found partner, the Indian's horizon widened out beyond all his dreams. He could travel as fast as the wind and as far. He could follow the buffalo; wherever they went, he went.

But after a while killing only one buffalo at a time seemed small sport. Contests were held to see who could kill the most with the fewest arrows. One chieftain shot sixteen bulls with seventeen arrows!

Sixteen bulls with seventeen arrows . . .

Day by day buffalo hunts grew wilder. More were slaughtered than ever before, and the herds dwindled and dwindled until they were almost gone. But the loss of the buffalo was only one factor in the decline of the Indian. The white man's greed for land made him encroach on Indian villages, taking over their vegetable patches and their hunting grounds.

When the Indians objected by firing the prairie grasses and stampeding the white man's horses, the government in Washington sent troops of cavalry to subdue them. Year after year, more and more troops came—charging the Indians, attacking them, disarming them. And cruelest of all, they took away their horses. Only then were the Indians beaten and forced back and squeezed into barren, desert lands.

The best of the Indians' horses were kept by the cavalry and a few were sold to the settlers. But many went free, and these became the feral horses. Like their wild relatives they formed into bands, roaming from one grazing ground to another. They drifted as far north as Canada and as far east as the Mississippi River.

While this drama was taking place in the West, the picture was changing in the East, too. English, French and Dutch colonists along the Atlantic seaboard were importing different types of horses—big brawny beasts for tilling the land, tall rangy horses for the sport of racing, and quiet saddle horses for transporting men and belongings. Gradually over the years the colonists and their horses pushed westward, even to the Mississippi and beyond.

And so, by the end of the nineteenth century, there were many, many different kinds of horses scattered all over the continent of America.

The Hot Bloods

There are a bewildering number of breeds of horses in the world today—more than sixty. Let's talk about the best known so that we can have the thrill and satisfaction of recognizing each one at a glance.

All modern breeds were developed from two strains: the big, heavy, cold-blooded horses and the small, swift, hot-blooded ones. From these, man bred horses bigger or smaller, heavier or lighter, according to his needs. To understand the present types we have to think back again to the two kinds of war horses that clashed in Europe when Charles the Hammer and his Franks fought the Moslems in that great Battle of Tours.

The Franks were mounted on their big, cold-blooded Flemish horses, which later became known as the Great

Horses of the Middle Ages. They *had* to be bred big to carry a knight wearing a heavy coat of mail, an iron helmet and breastplate. The horse, too, was covered with mail. Only his legs were free. He was indeed a Great Horse to maneuver under such a burden.

In direct contrast, picture the delicate, hot-blooded Arabians of the Moslems. They were small-boned, streamlined, and swift as the gazelle. Even in battle they could travel fast, for their riders were naked of trappings and wore only flowing white robes. From the blood of these desert horses, with cold blood intermixed, man has created all of the light breeds—the racers and the saddle horses.

Of course, the blood of one strain really isn't any colder or hotter than the other. It is mainly their temperaments that differ. The large European horse is generally calm and steady, while the smaller Oriental is fiery and spirited. This division of horses into the hot-blooded and the cold-blooded makes it easier for us to understand how man could emphasize certain characteristics to create breeds for his own purposes.

Let's begin with the Arabian and then the Thoroughbred, for they are the only true hot-blooded horses in the world today.

THE ARABIAN

Purest of all Breeds

The Arabian is the oldest and purest of horses. But he may not have come from Arabia! Where he originated we do not know. Some say it was in the mythical "land of speculation" and let it go at that. Others believe that early traders brought their finely made horses from the Tigris and Euphrates valleys to the northern coast of Africa.

But we do know it was in Arabia that these small, fleet horses were carefully bred and the strain kept pure. Mohammed and his men were mounted on Arabians as they conquered tribe after tribe in their big crusade.

These Moslems preferred a mare to a stallion. The lucky man who owned one regarded her with fierce devotion and

A young competitor rides in Arab costume

jealousy. Without her he was a pauper; with her he was rich. He could go to war, he could hunt, he could roam from one oasis to another. Not for any price would he sell her. He could only give her away, and this was the supreme sacrifice for friendship.

The finest Arabian horses were called *Asil,* meaning "pure-bred," and their ancestry could often be traced for eight hundred years. There were, of course, many mongrels which could be bought for a song, but they were scorned and called *kadisches,* impure in blood.

It is strange that in a desert country so unfriendly to the needs of horses there developed a type of such speed and stamina. Or is it strange? Perhaps the very scarcity of food, the searing rays of the sun by day, the bitterness of the winds by night, the long distances between water holes—perhaps these forced into being a tough, wiry horse able to travel long miles without water. At the end of the day his meager reward was often nothing more than a measure of barley chaff and a handful of dried dates. Or it may have been a drink of camel's milk which his master shared with him, as he did the comfort of his tent.

This close association with man developed in the Arabian horse a gentle disposition and an intelligence which still characterize him. He is swift and courageous, yet obedient as a household pet.

Of all horses the Arabian is considered the most beautiful. His body lines, from the graceful arch of his neck to the high carriage of his tail, are so distinctive that you can spot him by this symmetry alone. His head is small and delicate, with a broad forehead and a profile dish-shaped below the eyes. It tapers into a muzzle so small that it is said he can drink

Amon Carter Museum of Western Art; Fort Worth, Texas

1 *"Bronco Buster"* by Frederic Remington (1861-1909)

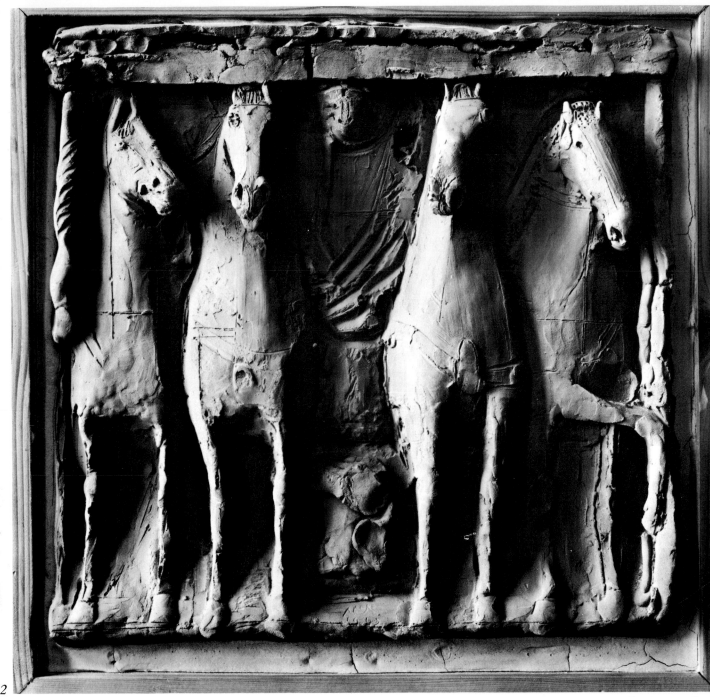

3

"*Quadriga*" by Marino Marini (1901-   )

Greek Attic Vase, 543-530 B.C.

(opposite, above) "*Racehorses*" by Edgar Degas (1834-1917)
"*Riderless Racers at Rome*" by Théodore Géricault (1791-1824)

Courtesy, Museum of Fine Arts, Boston. S. A. Denir Collection

The Walters Art Gallery

6   *"Mares and Foal"* by George Stubbs (1724-1806) (below) *"Regents Park"* by John Ferneley (1781-1860)

7

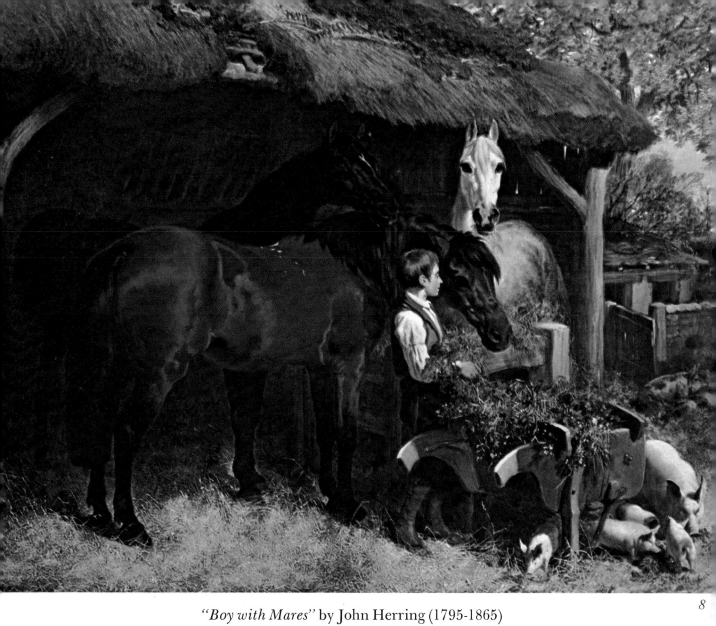

"Boy with Mares" by John Herring (1795-1865)

8

Illustration from *"Doctor Syntax"* by Thomas Rowlandson (1756-1827)

9

"Battle of San Romano" by Paolo Uccello (1397-1475)

11   *"Polish Rider"* by Rembrandt (1606-1669)

12

Alte Pinakothek, Munich

13

"Abduction of Rebecca" by Eugene Delacroix (1798-1863)

"The Lion Hunt" by Peter Paul Rubens (1577-1640) (opposite, below)

14

"The Knight, Death and the Devil" by Albrecht Dürer (1471-1528)

"Notre Jeanne (Our Saint Joan)" by Georges Rouault (1871-1958)

"Don Carlos Balthazar" by Diego Velazquez (1599-1660)

A small, delicate head and graceful neck mark the purebred Arabian

from a teacup. His eyes are large and wide apart. Usually they are ringed with black, giving them a luminous quality like a woman wearing eye shadow. His ears are small and lively, and often their tips point inward. The true Asil always has a satiny black skin, although his coat may be bright chestnut, light gray, or bay. His tail is not very long or thick, but because it is naturally set on high, it looks full and flowing.

As a pleasure riding horse, as a cow pony or parade horse, the Arabian is at his best. Today in America he is so well loved that there are more Arab horses here than in all of Arabia, Turkey, Persia, Syria and India put together.

The Arabian is the true aristocrat of the horse kingdom, and his blood introduced into other breeds gives them spirit, stamina, and speed. He is the fountain source of quality.

THE THOROUGHBRED

Race Horse Supreme

Man has loved the sport of racing ever since the first Olympic Games were held in Greece three thousand years ago. The biggest event then was the four-horse chariot race twelve times around the Hippodrome. Yet until recently there was not a horse in all the world bred solely for speed.

Steeplechasing at Belmont Park

The creation of a running horse is credited to England. Early in the eighteenth century the English imported three hot-blooded desert stallions. Their names are worth remembering—the Byerly Turk, Darley's Arabian, and the Godolphin Arabian. All three were small, almost pony size, but they were swift and *prepotent*, which means that their unique characteristics were handed down to their sons and daughters.

When these little desert Arabians were mated to the bigger English mares, the colts were strongly marked with Arabian qualities. In fact, their speed was intensified, for the youngsters could travel even faster than their Arabian sires. With each generation the colts increased in height, almost an inch for every twenty-five years. By 1850 they stood a full six inches taller than the three imported stallions. The longer legs, of course, meant a longer stride and faster time.

And so a new breed was created, the English Thoroughbred. His pedigree was carefully traced back to one or more of the three royal stallions. Today in England, America, or anywhere in the world the test of a Thoroughbred is still this ancestry.

Since the Thoroughbred is now a breed, the term must not be confused with the word *purebred*. We speak of a purebred Arabian horse, or a purebred Black Angus bull, or a purebred Beagle hound. But to a horseman a Thoroughbred is always a horse whose ancestry can be traced directly to the Byerly Turk, Darley's Arabian, or the Godolphin Arabian.

In looks, today's Thoroughbred is like, yet unlike, his Arabian ancestors. His body is slim, his face often dish-shaped and never Roman-nosed, his chest deep and broad, with big lung power. Even his colors copy the Arabian—seldom spotted, usually solid bay or chestnut, gray or black.

Thoroughbreds return from a workout at Hialeah racetrack in Florida

But he is a bigger horse in every way. And he can outrun the fleetest Arab. He can do the mile in less than two minutes, while other horses take four or more. He is the fastest horse in all the world.

His disposition, too, is quite different from the Arabian's. Instead of being mild as a lamb, he is often quick-tempered. Samuel Riddle, who owned the great Man o' War, admitted "he was a devil to break, a headache to handle, and a catapult to ride." But when trained, the Thoroughbred has the fierce determination of a lion and will finish the race even if it kills him.

He is brave and bold in other sports, too—in fox hunting and steeplechasing. These demand skill in jumping fences, leaping over ditches, sailing across streams. Steeplechasing is a form of racing originating in Old England, where the finish line was often a distant church steeple. It is even more exciting and far more dangerous than flat racing.

Of course, the Thoroughbred was created for the race track. Kings and sultans, butchers and bakers, oldsters and youngsters, people of all ages in all countries are fascinated by the Thoroughbred at the peak of his racing form. A three-year-old coming up from behind and galloping down the homestretch to win is a drama of courage and heart and speed.

10

The Cold Bloods

Let's talk now about the cold-blooded drafters, the heavy-boned horses from the Old World. We know most of them as Belgians, Percherons, Shires, and Clydesdales. Often they are called "The Big Four of the Draft World."

They are all descendants of the Great Horse of the Middle Ages, but in the long years since then their role has completely changed. From carrying heavily armored knights into battle they were put to peacetime work—dragging logs, pulling plows, carting loads of merchandise.

These four drafters are much alike. They are all enormous blocky horses, each weighing about a ton. Their feet are big, their shoulders, thighs, and legs bulge with muscle; they are the very picture of power.

THE BELGIAN

Champion Puller

Of all the heavy breeds, the Belgian is perhaps the most popular in the United States. He is a huge, muscular fellow, the chunkiest and strongest of the Big Four. He is a direct descendant of the Great Black Horse of Flanders. Originally he was pitch black like his ancestor of the Middle Ages, but now he is more apt to be chestnut or sorrel.

His mane and tail set him apart from the others. They are a beautiful blond color, called flaxen.

At county fairs the Belgian is the one that usually wins the log-pulling contest. With short legs his body is low to the ground and nearer to his work. This makes it easier for him to start pulling. First he digs in with his forefeet; then his strong hindquarters give the propelling power.

Big and mighty as he is, he has a gentle disposition. He takes the bridle and harness as calmly as he accepts sunshine and rain. In fact, a well-trained Belgian can easily be led by a small child with a piece of string for a halter rope.

Belgians—the brawniest of the drafters

Lively Percherons are favorites in the circus ring

THE PERCHERON

Pride of France

The Percheron takes his name from the rolling countryside
in France known as La Perche. The fields are rich in clover
and alfalfa and a pealike herb called "holy hay." Apple trees
dot the land and the whole province is laced with clear
streams. No wonder the Percheron grows to be a giant of a
horse, and a sprightly one at that.

Whatever he does, he does with spirit. Even in Old France when he pulled a loaded stagecoach, he trotted at a fast and jaunty pace. Now when he pulls a plow in our hilly northern states, his stride is quick and even graceful. And when he performs in the circus, he can dance or roll the barrel as skillfully as any two-legged acrobat.

Everything about him is massive, except his head. It is almost Arabian. Does this surprise you? But remember again the Battle of Tours. It took place not far from La Perche, and the victorious Franks captured many fine Arabians as prizes of war. Over the years these small hot-blooded horses interbred with the big native strain and stamped them forever with certain traits. The finely shaped head of the Percheron, his usual gray color and, more important, his gaiety and blithe spirit all show his Arabian ancestry.

THE SHIRE

Colossal English Drafter

Tallest, heaviest and hairiest of all breeds is the great English Shire. Frequently he weighs a ton before he is two years old.

He is an easygoing fellow, plodding and nodding along at his work. But with his tremendous power he gets things done in spite of himself. He moves slowly and methodically, except when it comes to nose-diving into his feed bag.

Next to his monstrous size, his "feathers" are the quickest way to recognize the Shire. These are thick shags of hair growing below his knees and hocks, giving his legs protection

The massive Shires are the biggest of the drafters

against barbed wire, sharp grass and ice.

His ancestry goes back to the Great Horses of Flanders who were brought to England and bred to native mares. The offspring was a powerful animal, the Old English Black Horse. Later he became the national draft horse of England and was renamed "Shire" from Lincoln*shire* and Cambridge-*shire,* where he was bred. Although he resembles his black ancestor in size and form, his color is usually bay or brown.

In America the Shire is often used to improve or "grade up" our smaller work horses. This crossbreeding is highly successful. It produces a "grade horse," a drafter of strength but more moderate in size and with fewer feathers. Shires, both grade and purebred, are still at work in our western states—logging, tree-farming, and in winter hauling heavy loads of hay to far-ranging cattle.

THE CLYDESDALE

Stylish Stepper of Scotland

The Clydesdale is the pride of Scotland, his home the open meadowland watered by the River Clyde. He is the only

The Clydesdale is the most stylish of the Big Four, at work or in the show ring

drafter used in Scotland. Even today contests are often held there to see which Clydesdale team can plow the fastest and the straightest.

How can we tell the difference between the Shire and the Clydesdale—especially since they are both the same brown or bay, and both have feathers on their legs and white blazes on their faces? There are at least four ways horsemen can tell.

First and most important is their action. The Clydesdale does not shuffle along as the Shire does; he steps right out as if he enjoyed the whole business of pulling the manure spreader or the plow. This "heather step" makes him the most stylish of the Big Four. Second, the Clydesdale is less bulky, not as blocky as the Shire. Third, the feathers on his legs are not coarse, but silky fine. And fourth, he is more generously splashed with white. His legs are often white up to the knees and his whole face may be white too. Even his belly is often marked.

At show time the Clydesdale wears seven-pound iron shoes called Scotch Bottoms. They are plainly visible because of the clean lifting of the Clydesdale's feet as he trots his heather step.

Today for many boys and girls the mere mention of the Clydesdale brings to mind that exciting moment at the Fair when a six-horse hitch swings briskly into the ring, with leg feathers swishing and feet keeping time to the jingle of their harness bells.

Fast and sure-footed, a Quarter Horse heads off a steer

The Warm Bloods

Besides the cold-blooded horses and the hot, there are the warm bloods, which are a mixture of the two and show a blending of their characteristics. They are called the light breeds, and each type has been bred for a specific purpose. The group is a big one, including pacing and trotting horses, walking horses, three- and five-gaited saddle horses, stock horses, and some double-duty horses.

While one breed did not follow another as Monday follows Sunday, it may be easier to understand today's horses if we learn about the older breeds first.

THE HACKNEY

High-Action Trotter

In early England when roads were hardly roads at all, there

was a lively cart horse known as the Old Norfolk Trotter. He was a handsome, robust fellow, and as he trotted over the mudholes, he picked his feet up high as if he scorned such things as puddles and bumps. This high action became his trademark.

When the sons of Darley's Arabian were mated with the Old Norfolk Trotters, a new breed of horse was born. He was muscly and round-barreled as the trotter, yet there was a new elegance about him. The head was finer, the ears smaller, and the neck more gracefully arched. And, curiously, the knee and hock action was even higher.

Horsemen quickly recognized that here was a fashionable new type of horse for pulling the English hackney coaches. And it was these coaches, of course, which gave him his name.

Knees high, a sleek pair of Hackneys show their animation and speed

You may think it odd that when railroads began to criss-cross the country the Hackney coach horse did not die out as a breed. His smart, quick step saved him for a new career. Horse trainers began grooming him for fairs and shows. And the more ribbons he won, the more they exaggerated his lively action.

Today a Hackney winner lifts his knees so high he almost bumps his chin whiskers. All manner of tricks in training are used. His shoes are weighted, rattlers are fastened to his ankles to make him step higher, and a rope-and-pulley device on his legs helps perfect the rhythm.

Aside from his brilliant performance, the Hackney can be recognized by his grooming. His long, bushy tail is usually docked. And when he steps into the show ring, his mane has been plucked and braided and his coat brushed to a gleaming brightness. He is quite the Beau Brummel of the horse world.

Today few horse shows are complete without harness classes for the Hackney. Most of them are for Hackney ponies, but in the important Devon Show held each year in Devon, Pennsylvania, sleek Hackney horses as well as ponies trot around the ring. They are like a pageant of the old coaching days. Sometimes the high-steppers are hitched to a phaeton driven by an elegant lady in a beautiful gown and picture hat. And sometimes they draw a two-wheeled gig with a high-hatted gentleman driver and a groom sitting straight as a ramrod alongside.

But to spectators who know Hackney history, the most exciting event of all is the class for matched Hackneys drawing a smart four-in-hand coach. It brings to mind the stylish Old Norfolk Trotter who long ago pulled carts and carriages over the rutted roads of rural England.

Over a short distance, Quarter Horses can beat a motorcycle

THE AMERICAN QUARTER HORSE

Cow Pony and Sprinter

For a quarter of a mile he can burn up the track. He can beat a Thoroughbred. He can even outdash a motorcycle. From a standing start he can reach top speed in two leaps. This is the American Quarter Horse.

Where does he get this burst of power? His deep sloping shoulders and his strong legs provide the punch. Notice the muscles of his forearms, like the biceps of a wrestler. Although he is blocky, he is quick and nimble on his feet. As the saying goes, "he can spin on a dime."

His career began in early Virginia, when the colonists wanted a horse for work *and* play. By crossing English pacers with Spanish jennets they developed a double-duty horse. He helped clear the wilderness and farm the land, and after his work was done he competed in match racing, the favorite outdoor sport of the times.

After the English Thoroughbred was imported, however, Virginians lost interest in their compact runner because the long-legged Thoroughbred always won. That is, after the first quarter-mile.

The Quarter Horse might have been neglected and forgotten if he had not been swept along in the westward march of our pioneers. In the grasslands of the Southwest the new settlers began raising cattle. As their herds grew and the ranges widened, it became too costly to fence them in. A good cow pony was needed, and the Quarter Horse stepped into his new role as if he had been bred for this alone.

Today no other horse can compete with him in rounding up cattle. Nor can helicopters, jeeps, or motorcycles take his place. They can't plow through bramble and briar, or pick their way along gully ledges, or climb mountains, or swim streams.

Nor do they have that amazing quality, "cow sense." The Quarter Horse can almost read the mind of a runaway steer. He anticipates which way it will turn, sprints ahead, and deftly blocks the path. And in cutting one out from the herd, he pounds alongside—twisting, doubling back, swerving, spinning on his hocks, outsmarting the shiftiest. Then, just as the cowboy's lariat tightens on the steer, he slides to a stop— bracing himself against the pull of a thousand pounds of bucking, bolting beef.

At branding time, when another horse would panic at the sight of fire, the Quarter Horse is cool and calm. He drags the little dogies—fighting, bawling, half crazy with fear—right up to the fire. Then he stands quietly by while they are branded.

His ability to start, stop, and turn quickly makes the Quarter Horse an excellent polo pony as well. And at rodeos he is unbeatable at barrel racing, bull dogging and calf roping. He is still a racer, too, still the fastest sprinter in the world.

The Quarter Horse can almost read the mind of a panicked calf

Turning "on a dime," the Quarter Horse is unbeatable at barrel-racing

But his real distinction is as a working cow horse. As one Texan remarked: "Until mountains dwindle to molehills and jeeps develop cow sense, the Quarter Horse will be my trusty partner."

THE MORGAN

All-Purpose Horse

In many ways the Morgan is very much like the Quarter Horse. He, too, runs a short explosion race. He even looks like the Quarter Horse, has the same kind of underpinning—short, sturdy legs with muscles big for his size. Their heads are alike, too, broad between the eyes and lean and bony, with little fox ears.

With all these similarities, how can we tell them apart? For one thing, the Quarter Horse is more chunky than the Morgan. And although they are alike in body color, the Morgan often has black legs and tail. His tail is his glory, very long and full. He often has hairy fetlocks, not as shaggy as the Clydesdale or the Shire, but noticeable enough to suggest some cold blood in his background.

Perhaps it is his trot that really shows the Morgan blood. It is low to the ground, quick, vigorous and short, so short that Vermonters say of him, "A Morgan can trot all day in a peck measure!"

Originally he was a work animal—a farm horse and log

Bred for all-round performance, a Morgan shows his jumping style

Morgans were originally work horses

puller. But on Sundays, groomed and polished, with the burrs combed from his tail and the harness brasses shining, he trotted in great dignity, taking his family to church.

Sometimes he is called the Justin Morgan horse for his founding father. The first Justin Morgan was a bay stallion, sturdy and courageous, a "big little horse." He, in turn, was named for his owner, Justin Morgan, a penniless singing teacher who traveled from school to school over the hilly roads of Vermont. The singing master became famous all over the world not for the songs he sang or the music he wrote, but because he owned this small bay stallion.

It was not until after the horse was dead, however, that his true worth was understood. Horsemen were amazed that his colts and grandcolts were exact replicas of him. Not only did they look like him, but they had his courage, strength and willingness to work.

When this prepotency was at last appreciated, people realized that a single horse had founded a whole new breed. Then they became curious about him, began probing and prying into his past. Who was his sire? Where did he come from?

Widespread searching revealed nothing. No letters. No written pedigree. Nothing but speculation and hearsay. From little clues and rumors a romantic story was built up. It may be true; it may not. It goes back to Revolutionary days when the English were occupying New York City. Colonel De-Lancey, a turncoat who had joined the British forces, was often seen dashing about town on a spirited Thoroughbred named True Briton. It was his custom to ride out to the edge of the city to visit his mother along about teatime.

An American farmer living nearby had frequently seen the Colonel and his handsome stallion. When this farmer's cattle were stolen by British soldiers, he stormed into the Colonel's presence, demanding payment. He even threatened to steal the Colonel's horse right from his mother's hitching post. The Colonel only laughed in his face. Later the farmer did capture True Briton, and galloped off to New England where he quickly sold him for a fancy price. And it was this stolen English Thoroughbred, so the story goes, who sired Justin Morgan.

Today Morgan horses are still the pride of the New England states, where they are the favorite mounts for long trail rides. But they are by no means limited to one section of the country. Morgan Horse Clubs are springing up all over the United States. And just as in the early days in Vermont, the Morgan is the same general-purpose horse, strong enough for work, fast enough for pleasure.

THE AMERICAN SADDLE HORSE

Five Gaited and Three

When our country was growing up, horses were of course the chief form of transportation. Rivers were stubborn; they went their own way. But a good horse went the rider's way. So everybody rode. Wagons were out of the question in the unbroken wilderness. It was horseback or nothing.

The destination of the pioneers was often a new homeland many miles away. Out of necessity they developed a horse that could travel long distances at an easy, steady pace with a rider or two on his back and a bundle of household goods besides. He was the American Saddle Horse. And he grew up with our country.

Like most Americans he was a mixture of nationalities. His blood was a melting pot, a blend of hot blood with warm and cold. From the Thoroughbred he inherited his fire and speed, from the Morgan his stamina and calm disposition, and from Spanish and French pacers his easygoing ambling gait.

As narrow trails gave way to passable roads, the burden of the saddle horse was lifted; it was transferred to wagons and carts. The hard life of the settlers, too, was eased. What they wanted now was more than a horse with a strong back and easy gaits. They wanted beauty and style and speed.

By selective breeding they were again successful—the Kentucky breeders especially. In the year 1838 an illustrious colt was born there, of an English Thoroughbred and an American Saddle Horse. He was called Denmark, and from him came the American Saddle Horse family as we know it today.

All its members are recognized by their distinctive gaits. The three natural gaits—walk, trot, and canter—are performed with great boldness and animation. In addition, the highly schooled saddle horse has learned two artificial gaits— a slow gait, which is usually a stepping pace, and the speedy rack.

The stepping pace is spectacular in its restraint. The horse is eager to go, but the rider holds him in, causing an instant's hesitation with every step. The action is high, with exaggerated motion of knees and hocks, yet very slow and controlled.

Bold action is the mark of the American Saddle Horse

The rack is the stepping pace at lightning-quick speed. The horse appears to be skimming along without any bodily motion at all. Yet his legs are strutting high, almost hackney-like. It is a grueling test of the horse's skill.

You can quickly tell a five-gaited Saddle Horse from a three-gaited even before he goes into the stepping pace or the rack. His tail is set high, artificially, and the hair must be long-flowing, the longer the better. Often it drags on the ground like a lady's train. The three-gaiter's tail is also set high, but it is clipped bare at the top, smooth as a shepherd's crook. Then it flows into a cascade of hair. His mane, too, is clipped, giving him a sleek, barbered look.

The American Saddle Horse is not bred solely as a show horse. He is popular with the whole family for trail riding and hacking across country. But in the show ring he is at his best. His action is fiery, his disposition is not. With precision and staying power he can rack on and on while the judges slowly ponder and the crowd goes mad with suspense.

No one enjoys the spotlight more than he. He has earned his title, "The peacock of the horse world."

Well-known trainer Earl Teater is the rider

THE STANDARDBRED

Harness Race Horse

Speed at the trot! All horses naturally want to gallop, but the Standardbred has learned to race at extraordinary speed without breaking into a gallop—even when urged to go faster, faster.

The distinguishing thing about the Standardbred is that his breed was founded on performance alone, not lineage as with the Thoroughbred. He was bred and trained to a standard of speed. And the United States set the standard.

In harness racing there are two gaits permitted—the trot and the pace. Usually each horse becomes expert in only one. In the trot the diagonal legs work together, but in the pace the two on the same side move as one. Pacing is not as natural a gait as the trot, and pacers often have to wear a kind of leg harness to hold them to their gait. This peculiar rigging is called hopples or sometimes "Indiana pants."

Up until 1840 harness racing was just a neighborly affair between owners of lively horses. But a New Yorker, happily named Jeremiah Trot, changed all this. He wrote a letter to the New York newspapers urging his fellow horsemen to organize a trotting club. Mr. Trot was highly successful, for soon a whole series of races was held in the New York area. From this small beginning, harness racing grew and spread. Fast oval tracks were built. Trainers were hired. The clumsy carts were cut down and given smaller, lighter wheels. Throughout the northern states harness racing became an exciting sport.

Thoroughbred racing, however, still ruled in the South.

At harness racing, the Standardbred is king

And it was to a great Thoroughbred ancestor, Imported Messenger, that the trotters owed their speed and gameness. Although he was noted as a running horse, his colts showed a surprising tendency to trot.

In succeeding generations Norfolk Trotter blood and also Morgan blood were introduced, and now the trotting tendency became fixed. The new breed was known as the Standard breed. Today a horse must be able to trot or pace the mile in two minutes and twenty seconds or less in order to qualify as Standard.

The world's most famous harness race is known as the Hambletonian. It is named in honor of a great-grandson of Messenger, Rysdyk's Hambletonian. His prepotency was so remarkable and he sired so many colts that 90 per cent of today's Standardbred winners trace their ancestry to him.

In looks the Standardbred is coarser and sturdier than his Thoroughbred ancestor. He has a longer head, and his ears are longer. He is usually stouter, too, and his legs more heavily boned. It is in his movement—the grand, bold, sweeping, reaching stride—that he gives the feeling of beauty.

The sport of harness racing is as American as red, white, and blue. The trainer may also be the driver, and he may be a young man or old—even in his seventies. There is no limit to his age, or weight. How different from the Thoroughbred's

Standard breeds on a New York farm

jockey, who is often a young flyweight, brought in as a complete stranger for just one race. The Standardbred horse, too, may still compete when he is "aged," but the Thoroughbred is often retired as a three-year-old. One famous trotter, Lady Suffolk, was still racing at the ripe old age of sixteen.

Today harness racing is enjoying a great new wave of popularity. There are more trotting tracks than ever before, and more Standardbred horses. Racing goes on by night and by day, in big cities and at country fairs alike.

Who says the horse-and-buggy days are gone?

THE TENNESSEE WALKING HORSE

For Show and Pleasure

After the War Between the States, the very battleground of Middle Tennessee became the cradle of a new breed. It had been a cavalry war with many horses dead, wounded and riderless. But with peace came a blood merger of the pacers of the South with the trotters of the North.

Before the war the Tennessee horse had been a comfortable ambler, the Plantation Walker. He would pull a plow or carry his owner up and down the endless rows of tobacco plants all day long. With the introduction of northern saddle-horse blood, however, his walk gained power and speed.

Like other breeds, the Tennessee Walking Horse had its own foundation sire. He was Black Allan, foaled in Kentucky in 1886 and taken to Middle Tennessee as a frisky, unpredictable colt. He came of a fine family. On his mother's side he went back to Justin Morgan, and on his father's side to Rysdyk's Hambletonian.

93

Hind foot ahead of fore foot, the Tennessee Walking Horse is noted for his smooth gait

With this background of trotting ancestors, it was expected that the trot would be his natural gait. His brother, Elyria, had already achieved an enviable mark; he could trot the mile in 2:25¼, slashing speed in those days of clumsy, high-wheeled sulkies and slow tracks. But instead of breaking Elyria's record, Black Allan absolutely refused to trot at all! He wanted only to walk and amble. And he was so loose-going and relaxed that he never made the mark of his brother.

Today hardly anyone remembers Elyria, but all Walking Horse owners know about Black Allan. The native mares that were bred to him were a mixture of Thoroughbred and Saddle Horse strains. Yet they produced colts that had a distinctive flat-foot walk, and a running walk not known naturally in any other breed.

The Tennessee Walking Horse is still used as a plantation

walker and for pleasure riding. But he has also been schooled for the show ring.

What is so special about him? How are his gaits different? Dr. F. L. Rogers, well-known show judge, describes the walk as eager and animated, as if the horse were hurrying homeward at twilight with oats in mind. Technically, it is a flat-footed walk, bold and square on all four "corners." And with each stride the hind foot oversteps the track of the front foot. This gives a natural gliding motion.

The running walk is the flat-foot walk in double-quick time with much greater overstride. The whole movement suggests a pitch, a pull, and a push: a pitch forward with front legs, a pull with the shoulders, and a push from the hindquarters. Yet the effect is anything but jerky. It is smooth and graceful. A good rider on a good horse can hold a glass of water in his hand without spilling a drop. This feat is often performed in shows and exhibitions.

The third gait is a rocking, rolling canter, a 1-2-3 beat. It is the gallop in slow motion, nice and "collected" and never increasing in speed.

In all three gaits the horse nods his head in perfect rhythm with his body. In fact, at one time he was called the Nodding Walking Horse.

The world's best of breed may be seen once a year in the national celebration held in Shelbyville, Tennessee. This is a week-long festival for all ages—foals, weanlings, yearlings, on up to aged horses. The climax of the show is the crowning of the Grand Champion Walking Horse of the World. And in all twenty-two years of the festival every champion has been fathered *and* mothered by descendants of old Black Allan, the little horse that refused to trot.

"MARES AND A FOAL" by George Stubbs, one of the great horse painters of 18th-century England

Points of the Horse

When you know how a horse is put together and can name his parts and how they function, you are on your way to becoming a horseman.

An experienced judge of horseflesh has the mind of an artist. At one sweeping glance he takes in the overall symmetry and quickly classifies the horse as weedy or well made. Then, if he is going to buy the animal, he studies it point by point. The amateur may have to do it the other way around —studying point by point first, and then drawing his conclusion.

Let's consider each point separately:

Head and Neck

A lean, small head contributes to the looks and balance of a horse. A heavy-headed horse may be all right for plowing a field or pulling a cart, but not for the hunt, the show ring, or pleasure riding.

Of all horses the Arab's head is finest. A line drawn from his forehead to his nostrils is not straight, but concave. Such horses are called dish-faced because the curve is similar to a saucer.

A convex profile is called a Roman nose, and while this is not a fault, it is more often found in heavy horses and never in the Arabian.

FOREHEAD   A broad forehead is good. It provides ample room for the brain and for the upper chambers of the nose, and it sets the eyes far apart, giving wider vision.

FORELOCK   The tuft of hair called the forelock is a natural watershed in rain or snow, and a neat whiskbroom for gnats and flies. Stallions grow big, bushy forelocks, which hang down well over their eyes.

A dish-shaped profile—an Arabian   *A Roman nose—a Clydesdale*

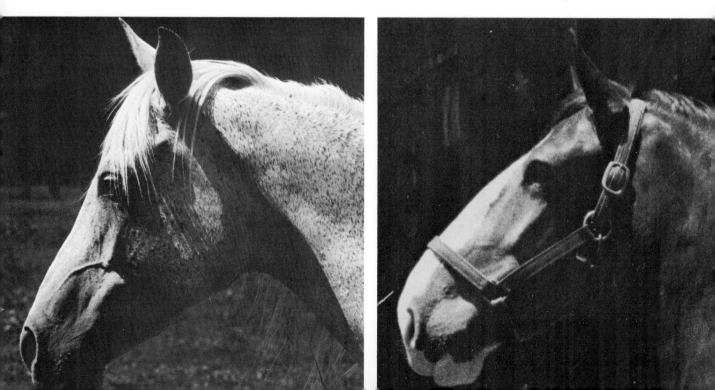

EARS   A small, foxlike ear can hear just as well as a big one, and is considered more beautiful. A horse can swivel his ears forward, sideward, and back, and thus pull in sounds from every direction. Often his ears give warning signals. They tell what he is about to do. A forward-pricked ear means a forward-going, happy horse. A flattened ear, turned back against the neck, usually foretells violent action—a kick, a bite, or a bolt.

EYES   The eyes of the horse are big and wonderfully constructed for keen vision in daylight or dark. They are like a wide-angled camera. While the pupils of your eyes are round, those of the horse are shaped like a long horizontal bar. He is able to see ahead, behind, and sideways all at the same time without the slightest turning of his head.

Except for the whale's, his are the largest eyes in the whole world.

In selecting a horse to buy, look for one with big, prominent, lustrous eyes. They are a sign of good health. And if they are wide-set, he is a safer mount because he can see farther behind and is less likely to shy at imaginary dangers.

Forelock—a Morgan

Wide forehead, small ears, large eyes—an Arabian

NOSTRILS Athletes, under stress, breathe largely through their mouth, while the horse can breathe only through his nose. The faster he goes, the wider he flares his nostrils. Therefore, it is good if he has big nostrils to begin with. Think how much more oxygen he can breathe in!

The rims of the nostrils of the draft horse are often whiskery, but in the Thoroughbred the hairs are delicate feelers, like the antennae of butterflies.

LIPS The lips of a horse are as sensitive as fingertips, especially the upper lip, which he uses in picking out his favorite wisps of hay or clover. Then he "lips" these choice pieces into his mouth. Thick lips are less skillful than thin lips.

CHIN Even though it is extremely small for his size, a horse does have a chin. In fact it will fit neatly into the cup of your hand.

JAW BARS You can see the horse's jaws at work as he grinds his grain into a soft mush. Old-timers used to place their fist up under the jaw to see if the bars were spread wide enough for plenty of grinding room. These bars are the racks

Flaring nostrils—racing Thoroughbreds

Thin lips, small chin—an Arabian

where the roots of the teeth are attached.

CHEEK A horse's cheek is different from the rounded human cheek. It should be as flat as your hand and without any fat at all.

THROTTLE Throttle is the horseman's term for throat, and it is located at the junction of the horse's head and neck. It should be a wide curve, not a sharp angle. A race horse, for example, takes in great gulps of air, and for him a flat throttle is a "must" to allow free breathing.

WINDPIPE Run your hand along the horse's windpipe below the throttle. When healthy, it reminds you of a flexible garden hose. Because food can go only one way—a horse cannot vomit—it is wise to feed him sliced apples or carrots instead of whole ones. Veterinarians tell of instances when a whole carrot or apple lodged in a horse's throat and only a quick operation saved him from choking to death.

NECK Draft horses have thick, muscly necks, while the neck of the Thoroughbred is fine. The horse with an extraordinarily long neck is "rubber-necked," and is difficult to control. A "ewe-necked" horse is a problem, too. He holds

Jaw bars—an Arabian   *Arched neck—a Lipizzan*

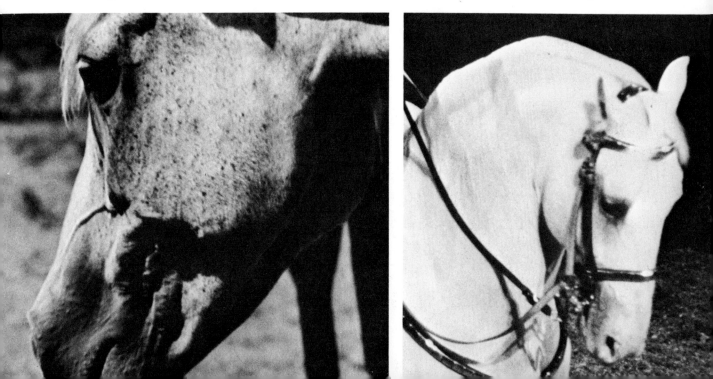

his head so high that he is almost impossible to manage. They both develop hard, insensitive mouths, and the rider, in trying to turn or stop them, has a tug of war of his hands.

POLL   The poll is comparable to the nape of your neck and is located immediately behind the horse's ears. It is a particularly sensitive spot. A sharp blow here can cause poll evil, a painful injury cured only by surgery.

CREST   The crest is the upper part of the neck from the poll to the shoulders. A good firm crest means that the horse is in fine fettle. The famed Godolphin Arabian was noted for his extraordinarily high crest.

Body

WITHERS   Where the shoulder blades nearly meet, there is a bony ridge called the withers. It is the highest point of a horse's backline, and should be smooth and gently rounded.

On a horse with well-shaped withers the saddle fits snug and secure, neither sliding nor turning. A flat-withered horse makes a poor mount. Instead of striding out and forward, he travels in an awkward, up-down motion. Mules and burros have almost flat withers. No wonder they can slide a saddle off, front or behind, hee-hawing at their own cleverness.

SHOULDERS   The shoulder blade is a thick flat piece of bone with muscles attached. The horse's front legs are lifted and extended by the action of these muscles. The longer the blade and the stouter the muscles attached to it, the longer his stride and the faster he can travel. It was Man o' War's strong, oblique shoulders that gave him fast action and a twenty-four-foot stride.

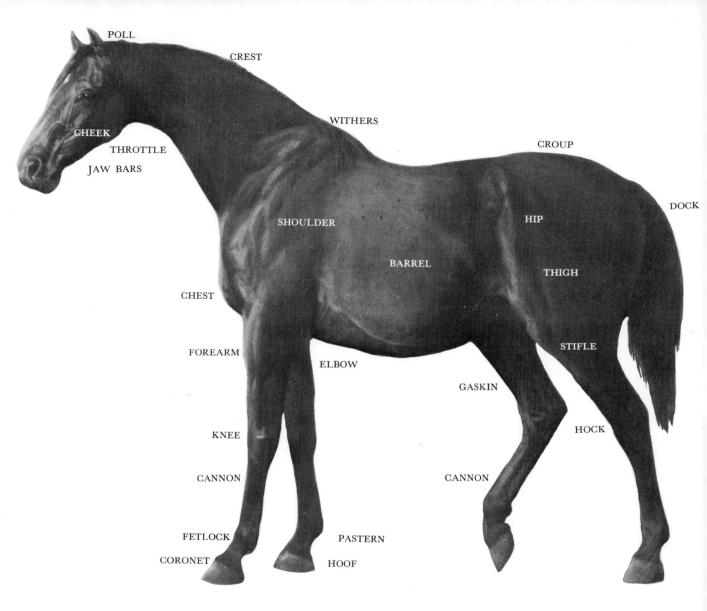

POLL

CREST

WITHERS

CHEEK

THROTTLE

JAW BARS

CROUP

DOCK

SHOULDER

HIP

BARREL

THIGH

CHEST

STIFLE

FOREARM

ELBOW

GASKIN

KNEE

HOCK

CANNON

CANNON

FETLOCK

PASTERN

CORONET

HOOF

CHEST The chest is the region of the body between the forelegs. In a newborn colt the legs are so close together he seems to have no chest at all. But as he grows in size and strength, it broadens and bulges with muscle. When he is full grown, a big chest provides good housing for heart and lungs.

BARREL The rounded body of the horse between the fore and hind legs is the barrel. It contains the rib cage and all of the digestive organs. If the ribs are not "well sprung" (curved like barrel staves), the horse is slab-sided, and this of course is a fault.

103

CROUP The highest portion of the hindquarters is the croup. For good conformation it should be slightly arched. A horse with a high, narrow croup is "goose-rumped," and one with a low, square croup is blocky looking. It is a happy medium, a gently rounded slope, which is desirable.

DOCK The dock or root of the tail is similar to our tail bone, but in the horse it is longer and has strong muscles, and he has control of it. He can move it from side to side, making a fly switch of his tail.

Hot-blooded horses carry their tails higher than do cold-blooded. The Arab's dock especially is held up high, and his tail flows well away from his body. The tails of other horses, except in action, usually hang limp.

Forelegs and Hind

The horse has a highly efficient set of leg muscles and bones and joints for moving forward with great speed. Not only are his legs bunched with big muscles above, but they are lengthened and strengthened below into powerful pistons that drive on and on and eat up the miles.

ELBOW AND STIFLE The elbow of the horse is a bony knob high on the back of his foreleg and corresponds to our elbow.

The stifle joint, similar to our knee, is at the upper part of the hind leg. And the thigh and hip, above this joint, are housed within the body.

FOREARM AND GASKIN The forearm is the muscular part of the front leg below the elbow. A long forearm means a long forward reach and a big striding horse. The hunter-jumper needs strong forearms as there is great strain in leaping brooks and brush. The draft horse, too, needs brawny forearms for pulling heavy loads.

The gaskins of the horse's hind legs are like the calves of our legs. To give propelling power they, too, should be strong and sinewy.

KNEE AND HOCK   The knee of the foreleg corresponds, of all things, to our wrist. But the joint is not as flexible as ours; it can move only backward. When viewed from the front, a large flat knee is desirable.

The hock on the hind leg corresponds to our ankle joint and should be large and bony. The knob that you see is one of the bones of this joint and really is the horse's heel. This shows how long and perpendicular his foot is, for this "heel" bone is high above the ground at all times. In fact, the word hock comes from the Old English "hoch," meaning "high."

CANNON   The cannon is a single bone directly below the knee or hock. It is called the cannon because it is hollow and round, like the barrel of a cannon. This rigid bone

A tangle of legs—Thoroughbred polo ponies

takes constant punishment, for with every stride the whole weight of the horse comes down on his front legs. Muscles and joints can "give" with pressure, but solid bone cannot. While a horse's upper leg should be long, the shorter his cannon the better.

FETLOCK   The fetlock joint on both the fore and hind legs corresponds to our knuckles. The term "fetlock" comes from the words "feet" and "lock," and refers to the tuft of hair at the back of the joint. In draft horses it is shaggy and long, but in the light breeds it is scarcely noticeable.

PASTERN   The pastern is the part of the leg between the fetlock joint and the hoof. It corresponds to the bones of our middle finger. It is really two bones, an upper and a lower, with a joint between. These with their ligaments act as a shock absorber when the foot hits the ground.

CORONET   The coronet is a soft band, something like our cuticle, encircling the foot just above the hoof.

HOOF AND FROG   The hoof is comparable to the nail of our middle finger or toe. The horse really stands on tip-toe, on his middle toenail. The thicker and tougher it is,

Fetlock—a Clydesdale   *Flying hooves—polo ponies*   *Frog—a Quarter Horse*

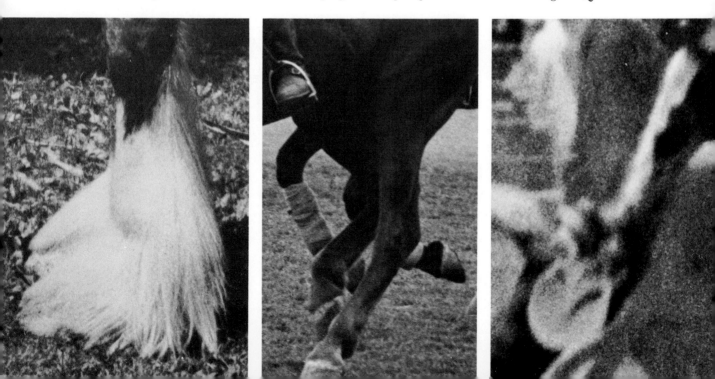

the better. It should be bell-shaped and smooth on the outside, and concave on the inside with a large prominent "frog."

The frog is a V-shaped mass of flesh in the middle of the sole of the hoof. It acts as a cushion with each step the horse takes, even when he is wearing shoes. Desert horses have better feet than horses reared in wet countries because the constant rasping of the sand keeps the hoofs filed down and the frog functioning.

CHESTNUTS AND ERGOTS The callous patches on the inner side of the horse's legs—just above the knees and below the hocks—are called chestnuts. They have no apparent use whatever, and no one seems to know if they ever did. Often they grow into rough, horny knobs which can be pared smooth until they look like the chamois patches on the elbows of a man's jacket.

Another curiosity is the ergot, a wartlike, pencil-shaped nubbin in the fetlocks. It can be easily twisted off so that it is practically invisible. This strange growth may be a remnant of the pad on little Eohippus' feet, for you recall that he walked on padded feet like a dog. The only horse that is apt to be free of ergots is the Thoroughbred. If he does grow any they are quite small. Both chestnuts and ergots, like callouses on people, can be trimmed without any pain at all to the animal.

Colors, Patches, and Spots

If we are riding across country and meet an old friend on a new horse, how nice to be able to say, "What a beautiful buckskin (or sorrel, or flea-bitten gray)!"

Or if we're at the races, watching the entries parade to the post, how nice to be able to say, "I like the chestnut first, and then the sandy bay."

To the beginner, color terms for horses may seem vague and puzzling, for they are not as distinct as the primary colors, red, yellow, and blue. But with a little study we may learn to know the common ones.

The Chestnuts

The chestnuts are the basic group of colors, and the tones

vary all the way from a yellow-gold to a deep orangey brown. The tail and mane of a chestnut horse are always the same color as the body, or lighter—even flaxen.

The liver chestnuts range from the color of liver with a yellow cast to a brown so dark it looks black.

The term sorrel is used to describe the yellow chestnuts; they may be anything from a light brassy hue to a deep orange.

The foal in the Stubbs painting (Plate 6, The Horse in Art) is a chestnut.

The Bays

By their tails shall ye know them! The distinguishing mark of a true bay is that he always has "black points"—that is, black mane and tail and frequently black legs. The color bay is really a long series of colors that build right on from tan to brown, with just a whisper of red in it, and on to a deep red-brown.

Sandy bay is light tan.

Mahogany bay is seal brown.

Blood bay is a shade between the tan of sandy bay and the brown of mahogany bay.

The Morgan mare and foal (Plate 16, The Breeds of Horse) are bays.

The Palominos

Palomino color can vary from pale honey tones to the golden sheen of a brand-new penny. It has been made famous by the golden parade horse of California. In addition to the brightness of his coat, the Palomino is known by his

1

The Arabian is the oldest and the most beautiful of the
breeds. He can be recognized instantly by his graceful
lines, his beautifully arched neck and his small delicate
head with its wide forehead and dish-shaped profile. The
Arabian above is a perfect example of the breed. He is
champion stallion Aahdin with his owner, Mrs. George
Rosenberg, in the saddle. Opposite, a yearling at the
Friendship Farm in Moline, Illinois, shows the typical
Arabian wide forehead and lustrous eyes.

3

4

6

Speed and stamina, inherited from Arabian and English ancestors, make the Thoroughbred an ideal mount for the grueling game of polo (opposite at bottom). They also make him the race horse supreme. Thoroughbreds can do the mile in well under two minutes, more than twice as fast as any other breed. Opposite at top is the greatest of them all—Kelso, five times Horse of the Year. Standardbreds (above) excel at another kind of racing; harness racing. There are two different gaits in harness racing; pacing and trotting. In pacing (at top), both legs on one side move in the same direction at the same time; in trotting (at bottom), the front leg on one side and the opposite hind leg move together.

The sturdy Quarter Horse is the most popular breed in America today. Bred as an all-purpose mount, he found a new life as the cowpony of the West (opposite). Quick wits, nimble feet, speed (he can outrace a Thoroughbred in a sprint) and an uncanny "cow sense" make the Quarter Horse champion of the range and the rodeo (right). Below is a perfect example of the breed, champion Cutter Bill, with his owner Rex Cauble.

9

The mighty drafters, the cold bloods, are descended from the medieval knight's war horse. A full-grown drafter is a giant among horses, weighing about a ton. The most popular breed in the United States is the Belgian. A two-horse team of Belgians can normally pull loads of 4,000 pounds; the record for the breed is 6,500 pounds. Opposite at bottom, a pair of Belgians heave at a wagon loaded with concrete blocks in a pulling contest at the Iowa State Fair. The Clydesdales, opposite at top, can be identified by their spritely "heather step." Another nimble stepper is the Percheron, whose lively character makes him a favorite in the circus ring. The six-horse team above is hitched to an antique circus wagon in the annual circus parade in Milwaukee, Wisconsin.

The warm-blooded, light breeds were each created for a special purpose. Hackneys (opposite, at top) were bred to pull the hackney coaches for which they were named. They can be recognized by their smart, high-stepping action. The American Saddle Horse (opposite, at bottom) is remarkable for his special gaits. Known as "The peacock of the horse world," he was bred for beauty, style and speed. Appaloosas were the war horses of the Nez Perce Indians. The mare and foal above come from a farm in Washington in the area where the breed first appeared.

14

15

The Morgan makes a sleek and spirited mount, yet he was originally intended to be an all-purpose horse, equally capable of hauling logs on weekdays, and of taking the family to church on Sundays. The Morgan mare and foal above live on the University of Vermont's Morgan Farm at Weybridge, Vermont, not far from the home of Justin Morgan, the penniless singing teacher who owned the founding father of the breed.

long-flowing silver mane and tail. Often he has white feet and ankles, too. But his body must be pure gold.

This golden color is so much admired and desired that in recent years Palomino fanciers have been crossing their Palominos with Arabian, Thoroughbred, Quarter Horse, and Saddle Horse strains to produce a horse beautiful in conformation as well as in color. The Palomino is now a breed. Golden Quarter Horses, golden Saddle Horses, golden Tennessee Walking Horses can be registered with two associations—the Palomino because of color and the Quarter Horse, say, because of breeding.

On New Year's Day, whether you are viewing color television or black and white, you can immediately recognize the Palominos in the Rose Bowl parade. They stand out unmistakably from the bays and chestnuts and blacks. Palomino is the one horse color everyone knows—expert and amateur, young folks and old, boys and girls alike.

Cutter Bill (Plate 9, The Breeds of Horse) is a Palomino Quarter Horse.

The Blacks

A truly black horse must be solid black, skin and hair both. To distinguish a black from a dark brown, look at the fine hairs on his forehead, muzzle, and legs. If they show any brown hairs at all, call him a dark liver chestnut. But if the hairs about the muzzle have a red tinge, he is a mahogany bay!

In reality most of the blacks are not coal black but are rusty black because their coats have been faded by the sun. Cowboys call them sunburned blacks.

The Grays

A gray horse is usually born a solid dark color, but his coat gradually whitens with age. Gray is not a true color but rather a mixture of white and colored hairs.

A flea-bitten gray is one with freckles of brown.

An iron gray has an abundance of dark hairs mixed with the white. In the Old West such a horse was called a Steel-dust.

A dappled gray has a variegated pattern of mottles, gray on gray.

Most celebrated among the grays are the beautiful Lipizzans of Austria. They are sooty black when born and become lighter each year until their coats are almost pure white. This snowy whiteness adds to the beauty of their performance as they pirouette and leap into space in their spectacular horse ballet.

Black at birth, Lipizzans become snowy white as they mature

The Albinos

An Albino horse is totally white from colthood to old age. He is the only true white horse with not a trace of color in his coat. Even his eyes are colorless and they are highly sensitive to sunlight and glare.

The White Horse Ranch in Nebraska founded a new type of white horse called the American Albino. His coat is clear white from birth, but unlike the true Albino his eyes are dark brown, dark blue or hazel, and they can adjust to sunlight and glare like those of any normal horse.

The founding sire was Old King, an all white circus horse who looked like an Arabian. Today his descendants have the general characteristics of the Arabian and are recorded in the American Albino Horse Club.

The Duns

The color dun has a faded look, as if a color had once been there, then faded out. It varies from a dull yellow to an ashy yellow.

The quickest and surest way to recognize a dun is by his stripes. He always wears a dark stripe along his spine and sometimes across his withers, and occasionally horizontal stripes on his legs.

Claybanks are the lightest of the group; they are sorrel or sandy bay in color, with the dark striping of course.

Buckskins are sandy bay but have the distinguishing stripes of the duns as well as the black manes and tails of the bays.

Mouse duns are liver chestnut or mahogany bay with the dun striping. In the darker, smokier shades, which resemble a house mouse, the stripes often seem to melt into the body color and you almost have to imagine them.

The Roans

Roan, like gray, is a mixture; it has a color base, salted with white hairs. But a roan colt is born roan, whereas a gray is born black.

The strawberry roan has a sorrel base.

The red roan has a base color of blood bay, and his lower legs are black.

The blue roan has dark body hairs which give a blue cast through the white; his lower legs, too, are often black.

The Paints or Pintos

Horses with patches or splotches of color on white are known as paints or pintos. Depending on the color of the patches they are called piebalds or skewbalds. If their patches are black, they are piebalds, and if any other color, they are skewbalds.

Paints vary in pattern all the way from an almost solid dark horse with only a few spots of white to an almost white horse with just a few spots of color.

The Appaloosas

Perhaps the most interesting spotted horse in all American history is the Appaloosa, the swift buffalo runner and war horse of the Nez Percé Indians of the Pacific Northwest. Among the paints he is unique. Instead of large splotches of brown or black, his may be either color, and generally

A paint Quarter Horse

they are no bigger than spatters of ink. Yet there is a kind of pattern to them. The spots seem to cluster over the rump.

(Plate 13, The Breeds of Horse, shows an Appaloosa mare and foal.)

But spots and patches and colors do not make the horse. They are no mark of mettle or courage. No one of them is better than another. Happily, each owner thinks the color of his horse is the most desirable. There is an old, old saying that satisfies us all: "A good horse can never be of a bad color."

Horseman's Talk

Every art or science or trade has a language all its own, a kind of special vocabulary. The world of horses is no exception. Newcomers to this world often call all members of the equine family simply horses. But the expert uses the particular term that fits the particular horse. For example, he speaks of a baby horse as a *foal*. And if he wants to specify its sex, he describes it as a *filly* if it is a female, or a *colt* if it is a male.

Foals may also be called *sucklings* while they are still nursing. Then later on, when they discover that hay and oats are quite as delicious as mother's milk, they are known as *weanlings*.

There is a rule in the Thoroughbred world that the birthdays of race horses always fall on January first. Even though

117

A Morgan foal

a Thoroughbred colt may be foaled in the month of December, he is considered a *yearling* on January first. He may actually be less than one month old, or even one day old! For this reason breeders like to have a Thoroughbred colt arrive as early in the year as possible so that when he is a candidate for the Kentucky Derby in May he will be over three years old instead of under. Owners of other breeds are not as particular about foaling dates; they often use a horse's real birthday.

By the time he is three, the colt is a *stallion*. Some stallions are altered by operation so that they can never become fathers. They are termed *geldings,* and they are quieter, more easily handled than stallions, and usually make safe and sensible saddle horses.

A filly is still a filly until the age of three, when she becomes a *mare*. After she is mated and has foals of her own, she is a *dam*, and if she is chosen to produce a foal year after year, she is a *broodmare*.

Telltale Teeth

All horses—mares, stallions, and geldings—are *aged* horses after they are nine years old. How can we tell their age? By ignoring the old motto, "Don't look a gift horse in the mouth." For it is the teeth that give away age.

When he is "rising three," the horse's permanent teeth begin to push out his baby nippers. They appear in pairs, first the two center teeth in each jaw, then a year or so later the ones on each side of them, and finally the corner pairs. These twelve front teeth are the grass-tearing *incisors*, and they are curiously marked. On the cutting surface of every one you can see a tiny hollow or *cup*.

At the same time that the horse is growing his permanent incisors, he is also getting his grass-grinding cheek teeth or *molars*. By the time he is five years old he has a "full mouth," twelve incisors in front and twenty-four molars in back.

A horse's teeth have a great advantage over ours. As he goes on maturing and eating his way through life, his teeth wear down from use just as ours do; but to make up for it his continue to grow out! In this wearing-away process the cups in the incisors gradually disappear. At six or seven, the cups in the center pair of lower front teeth have worn away;

119

and then at about yearly intervals the other cups disappear, two by two. Then the same wearing-away process occurs in the upper teeth until by the age of eleven or twelve all of the cups are gone. By noticing how many remain, an experienced horseman can estimate a horse's age.

Even after twelve, experts can judge age by studying the length and slant of the incisors. The longer and more sloped they are, the older the horse.

As for the grass-grinding molars, they also wear away and grow out. Sometimes they develop very sharp points which can gouge a horse's cheek or tongue. Horses of all ages should see their dentist once a year so that these jagged edges can be filed smooth, thus keeping the teeth useful. Otherwise a horse might starve, even though he is fed the plumpest of oats! This filing job is called *floating* because the file moves gently on the cutting surface of the teeth. Floating does not hurt the horse at all; it just frightens him the way the dentist's drill makes people uneasy.

Some horses, especially those with neglected teeth, are often gaunt and worn out by the time they are ten. Others have a sleek coat, bright eyes, sound limbs, and good wind well beyond this age. The police horses of Cleveland and New York, for example, are often on daily duty even in their twenties. And Lipizzan stallions, because of their excellent care, have been known to perform their difficult ballet routines up to the age of thirty.

Identification Tags

Colts or fillies, weanlings and yearlings, two-year-olds and four-year-olds, and aged horses—these are the stages of horse life. But all through the years nearly every horse has some marking of his own which never changes. Markings have a special vocabulary, too. As one equestrian says:

Stars and stripes and stockings and socks
Are as important to know as withers and hocks.

A *star* on a horse's forehead is seldom star-shaped. It may be almost any shape, or no shape at all—just a blob of white. Occasionally it takes the form of a crescent or a diamond, but it is still called a star.

The Arabian leader, Mohammed, prized horses with a star above all other markings. He called it a sign of glory and good fortune. He and his tribesmen often named their colts for this mark, and the custom is still popular today. Among the Thoroughbreds we find Morning Star, Lucky Star, Starlight, Shooting Star, North Star, and so on.

The tiniest marking on a horse's nose is a *snip*. It can be pink or white, and is usually found between the nostrils.

A white band down a horse's face is a *blaze*. This is so distinctive that the name "Blaze" crops up many times in storybook horses and in real life. One of the fleetest horses

Star . . .   *blaze . . .*   *and baldface*

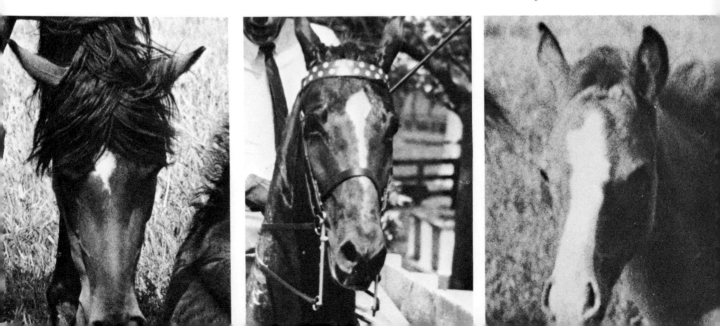

which ever ran on the English turf was a famous stallion named Blaze, who sired many blaze-faced Thoroughbreds.

On some horses there is just a white line down the nose, thin as a pencil. It is called a *race* instead of a blaze. Old-timers may refer to it as a *reach* or a *streak* or a *stripe*.

A *bald-faced* horse may be white from forehead to muzzle, including the entire front of his face. Our American Indians had many "Bald Eagles" and "Bald Chiefs" among their paint ponies.

Leg markings are also good identification tags—a white coronet or a white heel, a white pastern or fetlock. Most common are *socks* and *stockings*. The socks are short, of course, while the stockings reach well up to the knee or hock.

Now that you have mastered both color and markings, you can be as explicit in describing your horse as one of De Soto's men who wrote back to Spain: "My horse is good beyond words. He is a pitch-hued chestnut, his left hind foot white-stockinged, the blaze on his face coming down so low he appears to drink it." If this had been written today, the phrase "left hind foot" would probably read "*near* hind foot." For in America it is the custom to mount a horse from his left side, the near side. The horse's right side is the *off* side. In other words, off and near simply mean right and left.

Socks . . .   *. . . and stockings*

Misty—a Chincoteague pony

Universal Talk

Not quite so simple is the term for measuring a horse's height. At a glance a seasoned horseman will drop a mental plumb line from the top of a horse's shoulders to the ground. His conclusion may be something like this: "That stallion is a tall fellow; he must be 17:2 at least." If we translate this jargon, we learn that the stallion is 17 *hands* high, plus two

123

inches. A hand is four inches; so we multiply 17 by 4 and add the 2 inches, which gives a total of 70 inches. Therefore, this stallion *is* tall; he measures 5 feet 10 inches from the bottom of his hoofs to the highest point of his withers.

It is interesting to know that all over the world horses are measured in hands. The dollar changes everywhere, and gallons and weights vary too. But in India, China, England, America, everywhere horses are measured in hands.

And it is exciting that no matter how much machinery replaces the horse, the work it can do is still measured in *horse*power—even in this space age. The first rocket that lifted the first American into outer space had a weight-lifting booster of nearly a million horsepower. Horsepower has become a world term, translated into French, German, Swedish, Italian, Spanish, and Yiddish.

And the feeling which man has for his horse is universal. He respects machines. He knows they are tougher than horses, can stand heat and cold better, and they do not have to be watered and fed when they are idle. But with all their efficiency they cannot give one vital thing, companionship.

The jeep or automobile doesn't whinny in gladness or in anticipation of breakfast when you come out to the garage in the morning. And you can't smack it on the fender and tell it to move over. And it doesn't care whether you ever take a ride or not. And it doesn't lip carrots from your hand or nip your jacket in fun or slobber water over your clean shirt. Machines have about as much warmth as a refrigerator. And that is why the horse is still a part of our lives and will live on. He was here millions of years before man came upon the earth, and if the cycle is completed he may still be thundering across the world long after man has vanished.

Index

MARGUERITE HENRY is one of America's most distinguished and best-loved authors. She won the Newbery Medal for *King of the Wind,* her book about the Godolphin Arabian. She has written eleven other books about horses, among them *All About Horses* (Random House), *Misty of Chincoteague, Album of Horses,* and *Justin Morgan Had a Horse.*

WALTER OSBORNE has had a varied and creative career—as newspaper editor, art director, author and photographer. He has written and illustrated, among others, *Horse Racing* and *The Treasury of Horses,* and is one of the three American photographers represented in the Permanent Poster Collection at the Museum of Modern Art. *Marguerite Henry's All About Horses* is his first children's book. Mr. Osborne now lives in New York City.